THE VODKA IN THE PUNCH
AND
OTHER NOTES FROM A LIBRARY SUPERVISOR

BY NANCY POLETTE

LINNET BOOKS ● 1975

Library of Congress Cataloging in Publication Data

Polette, Nancy.
    The vodka in the punch, and other notes from a library supervisor.

    Bibliography: p.
    Includes index.
    1. School libraries—Administration. 2. Instructional materials centers—Administration. I. Title.
Z675.S3P57   025.1   74-31237
ISBN 0-208-01494-2

© 1975 by Nancy Polette
First published 1975 as a Linnet Book,
an imprint of The Shoe String Press, Inc.,
Hamden, Connecticut 06514

All rights reserved

Printed in the United States of America

Contents

Preface   5
1 / Life with School Administrators   7
2 / The Vodka in the Punch—or Never Entertain a Volunteer   28
3 / Eureka! A Staff of Twelve   43
4 / Uncle Sam Hates Library Supervisors: Bids, Budgets, and Bureaucracy   66
5 / All This and the Censors Too!—or Life in a Conservative Community   97
6 / The Fall from the Ivory Tower: The Supervisor as a Media Specialist   116
Appendix
    Criteria for Evaluating Research Centers *by Reva Butson*   131
    Toward Better Service *by Thelma J. Estes*   138
Selected Bibliography   147
Index   151

Preface

Much has been written about school library administration. The literature, however, is less abundant concerning the exhausting, frustrating, exciting, and rewarding job of the school library supervisor. These brave souls, who were set adrift on stormy bureaucratic seas without a compass in the years following ESEA 1965, found that in having to sink or swim they not only learned to swim, but eventually became champions. Every school library supervisor who has nursed an infant program to the stage where it can stand with pride, knows that the means by which this feat was accomplished were sometimes devious, often humorous and frequently less than orthodox.

The Vodka in the Punch and Other Notes from a Library Supervisor is an attempt to draw a composite picture from the experiences of many district-wide directors of library/media programs. Portraits drawn of administrators, librarians, media directors, teachers, volunteers, parents, and students are admittedly exaggerated to point out specific problems clearly and are in no way intended to refer to any specific individual or school district. When actual programs are described in the book, they are specifically identified by director and/or school district.

While the book is not a definitive study on supervision, it is a sharing of thoughts and ideas which may prove to be of help to the new school library supervisor and of reassurance to the experienced supervisor who has long had a desire to see some of her thoughts echoed by others in the hope that the sharing of problems may serve to bring about speedier solutions.

1
LIFE WITH SCHOOL ADMINISTRATORS

Teenage children and long suffering wives share one thing in common with school librarians. Each feels that he is without doubt the most misunderstood person in God's Universe. Teenagers are certain they are not listened to by parents; wives have rarely been listened to by their husbands; and many librarians feel that their only recourse to obtaining the school administrator's ear is to break down his office door, sit on his lap, grab an ear in each hand, and SHOUT. After a few years of working with school administrators at the district level, one discovers that shouting is rarely effective, although some desk pounding and a few choice words added to one's vocabulary (i. e. *damn it to hell!*) can, at times, bring desired results. Since library supervisors are generally female and school administrators are usually male (women's lib notwithstanding) other approaches to achieving one's goals might be taken; however, lest the reader be disappointed, the notes of this supervisor shall be confined to the "office door open, secretary present" approach.

While levels of command vary somewhat in large school districts, they are generally confined to (moving from the top down) the Board of Education which approves district policy, and incidentally, hires and fires; the Superintendent of Schools; two or three or more Assistant Superintendents who control the areas of finance, curriculum and personnel; a director of special services; and one or more principals for each secondary and elementary school. This array of administrative expertise is on hand to supervise the activities of several hundred teachers who, in turn, are charged with directing the activities of several thousand students. Added to this educational melting pot are enough "interested patrons" to make one think that each child came forth from the efforts of more than one set of parents.

The Library Supervisor: A Portrait

This somewhat mixed conglomeration of people, all involved in one way or another in the business of education, is also involved both directly and indirectly with the business of media centers. Thus to deal with these diverse elements, the library supervisor must encompass qualities that go far beyond those suggested in standard library school textbooks.

For starters the list of qualities might include:

> The courage of Sir Gawain
> The golden tongue of Daniel Webster
> The curiosity of Madame Curie
> The imagination of H. G. Wells
> The writing skills of Dante
> The public relations of Dale Carnegie
> and the ability to teach Willie Loman all he should have known about salesmanship!

Proof that this paragon does exist in considerable numbers throughout the nation's educational complexes today can be found in the tremendous growth of elementary library programs in schools all over the country in the past ten years. While many would attribute this phenomenal growth of elementary media centers (long considered the stepchild in the library world) to the efforts of the Federal Government through ESEA II, the funds allocated by Congress for school library services could easily have been channeled into thumbtacks and workbooks for individual classrooms without the dedication, vigilance, and perseverance of thousands of school librarians. The advent of the Elementary and Secondary Education Act of 1965 did indeed create a need

Life with School Administrators 9

for library personnel at the elementary level. Overnight, librarians were promoted (or demoted, depending upon your point of view) to the job of library supervisor. Simply put, this gave the task of finding space, furnishings, acquiring and organizing materials, staffing, providing support services, and selling the elementary library/media program to administrators, teachers, students and parents to a single individual who, in all likelihood, was expected to perform this miracle not in one, but in five, ten, or twenty or more schools. That the job was accomplished is no small miracle.

Organizational Chart

BOARD OF EDUCATION

Asst. Supt. Business	Asst. Supt. Curriculum	Asst. Supt. Personnel
	Dir. Sec. Curriculum Dir. Special Projects Dir. Elem. Curriculum	
	Secondary Principals Elementary Principals	
	Library Supervisor	

The Politics of a School District

Anyone embarking on a district-wide project should thoroughly understand the politics of the educational system. He or she should also be well acquainted with a very important item called "channels." Webster defines a channel as "a straight or narrow sea between two close land masses." To steer from the channel would, naturally, put one on a collision course. On the other hand, any sailboat owner would agree that the shortest distance between two points is not always a straight line. When storm clouds abound, the objective is usually accomplished most easily by tacking or changing direction when the boat is close-hauled from the starboard to the port tack. By now the reader must be getting the message that while it is the Board of Education who makes the final decisions on new programs, policies, staff, and expenditures, one does not move directly from idea to boardroom. Any attempt to proceed on such a straight course would result in a continuation of one's course right out the school district doors, nevermore to return! Thus, one must follow channels no matter how immediate the need or great the idea.

Those who must first be convinced in order to get the program off the ground are the elementary principals, who in turn assist in getting the message to the director of elementary education who, assuming he has received the message properly, will relay it to the assistant superintendent and finally to the superintendent of schools who again, if sold on the program, will relay the recommendation for staff, funds, facilities, or whatever the current need may be, to the Board of Education.

Any major deviation from wending one's way through this political hierarchy will result in maintenance of the status quo. Lest one be overly encouraged in thinking there are only four levels to climb, he should remember the games played as a child with instructions to "take one step forward, four steps back." A close examination of step one will reveal the problem.

The Elementary Principals

In a school district with fifteen elementary schools, one will generally find fifteen elementary principals, each a past master at playing king of the hill. Having achieved the top of the hill (defined as the principal's office), each is understandably determined to remain there. Endorsing a new program is an excellent way of making educational waves, and thus it takes a knowledgeable, competent, and nonthreatening library supervisor to calm the troubled waters. To complicate the problem, each administrator is a unique individual, and no two can be approached in the same way. However, if one observes closely, many administrators can be cataloged and dealt with according to type.

Type One: *The Innovator*

The "innovator," also known as the "grandstander," makes a great show of initiating any new program. For

Life with School Administrators

the library/media center, he will immediately make available his largest broom closet and will have ten volunteers per day lined up to work before card stock is ordered. While at first glance this enthusiasm may seem a welcome change for the supervisor, she soon discovers that the program never moves any farther than this. Requests for additional funds or space and staff fall on deaf ears. All proposals made to the "innovator" must be presented from a public relations viewpoint. If the supervisor can show just how a particular idea may enhance the prestige of the principal or school in the eyes of the public, she may more easily obtain the support of the innovator.

Type Two:
The Budget Watcher

The "budget watcher" is wary of anyone, especially library supervisors, who might suggest how the school's budget for instructional materials might best be spent. A request for a card catalog (not considered unreasonable by the supervisor) is quickly countered by the suggestion that cardboard boxes can serve as well. All requests made by the supervisor must, if at all possible, stress *savings* in time, money or materials if they are to be granted.

Type Three:
The Nitpicker

The "nitpicker" can find a thousand reasons why an idea won't work. His actions have inspired the bard to write: "Nothing turns me off quicker than the administrative nitpicker!" Before presenting an idea to the nitpicker, every question and angle must be carefully thought out and alternative approaches developed.

Type Four:
The Fencesitter

The "fencesitter" can keep the supervisor waiting for the smallest decision for weeks on end . . . unless . . . circumstances can be contrived to shove him off the fence. The most effective means of dealing with the fencesitter is to obtain the support of his superior for an idea in order that he will feel safe in endorsing any new plan of action.

Type Five:
The Buddies
The "buddies" always work together. These generally consist of two or more principals who keep the phone wires hot between schools conferring on each decision until a consensus is reached. Great care must be taken to be consistent in presenting ideas to each of the buddies, beginning with the principal in this group with whom the supervisor feels she has the greatest rapport.

Type Six:
Mr. Agreeable
"Mr. Agreeable," usually new in his job, places his stamp of approval on any and all requests, with usually disastrous results when such requests come from opposing points of view. Mr. Agreeable, as a result of such indiscriminate behavior, either loses his job rather quickly, or does a rapid about face and reverts to one of the five types cited previously. One should avoid presenting any type of impulsive idea to this principal.

The Supervisor

However, assuming that the school district has been coerced via Uncle Sam's red tape into establishing the position of library supervisor, she then has one foot in the door. She has been hired! At this point, she calls upon those skills of Dante and proceeds to write, and write, and write. Since educators are for the most part visually oriented, if a goal, a policy, a procedure, a recommendation, or a statement is not down on paper (in triplicate) it does not exist. Thus, the supervisor who hopefully knows where she is going, must now define the policies, procedures, programs, and recommendations for the media center in writing to others.

Ideally, the development of basic goals for any educational program should be a cooperative effort of the supervisor, the librarians, administrators, and teachers to determine their concept of what such a program should be. However, such a determination usually reveals the following teacher-administrator concepts and attitudes concerning the elementary library/media center.

Life with School Administrators

Administrator Attitudes and Concepts	Interpretation
1. An elementary library is nice to have but we don't really need it.	I'd rather not be bothered.
2. If someone wants to put a library in my school that will be fine if a room is built on the school (since we don't have space); money is appropriated for materials (since my budget won't cover any additional expense); and a librarian is assigned to my staff who doesn't "bother" my teachers. After all, they have a busy enough day.	Don't expect any help from me or my staff.
3. An elementary library is a place to get books to "read for fun." It's nice to have, but doesn't the bookmobile serve the same purpose?	I will probably be criticized by patrons for adding frills to the program.
4. There isn't really any need to catalog or organize materials. It isn't a REAL library, you know.	My clerical staff is already overworked. I can't spare them for anything else.
5. I suppose I can see some merit to having a list of the books in the library. You want this on cards? My secretary can type a few for you in her spare time.	Someone at the Central Office may ask for a report.

6. These students already have a very full school day, but I will schedule each class for 30 minutes per week to get books. Do we really need a librarian? I have some mothers that can do an excellent job checking out books to children.

I would much prefer to see the money spent on a librarian's salary used for other purposes.

7. Reference skills? We've done a lot in reference in our school. Every room has a set of encyclopedias.

Who needs anything except an encyclopedia in an elementary school?

Teacher Attitudes and Concepts

1. Centralized libraries? What would I do with one?

2. It has taken me five years of saving PTA attendance prize money to buy 12 copies of *Charlotte's Web*. No librarian is going to get her hands on these, or any other books in my room!

3. Children learn in the library? Oh, no, they can't possibly learn unless I'm working right with them.

4. Children don't need all those fancy audiovisual materials. After all, in the

Interpretation

Teacher attitudes are generally the result of lack of experience with the library/media center. Changing these attitudes is a slow process but can be accomplished through hard work coupled with tactful suggestions.

I haven't learned a new teaching skill in twenty years and don't intend to start now.

elementary school reading is the most important thing. Besides, I could never learn to run all those complicated machines.

5. Well, I might have a few really advanced students who could spend *some* time in the library.

Much to the dismay of the idealistic new library supervisor, she discovers that these attitudes, far from being unusual, are most generally prevalent in school districts that have never known the benefits of a good library/media program. The ongoing task of the supervisor, then, is that of changing attitudes, while making as few waves as possible. It was noted earlier that in initiating action, one begins with the principals and works one's way up the ladder. The more subtle and devious task of changing attitudes can be undertaken at whatever level the supervisor happens to find herself at the moment. One of the best places to start is in the office of the director of elementary education since principals more quickly reflect the attitudes of their superiors than of the library supervisor, and teachers are most definitely influenced by the attitudes of their principals. Thus begins the era of desk pounding and memo writing.

The Superintendent of Schools (Two Models)

Model One: *The Closed Door Superintendent*

Without question the most important and influential person in any school district is the Superintendent of Schools. If one assumes that the Board of Education has placed its trust in the Superintendent, then his recommendations carry greater weight than those of any other individual. Hopefully, his recommendations are formed after a careful study of the proposals and ideas of other district employees.

As with principals, superintendents come in all sizes, shapes and attitudinal postures. Some "Garbo type" superintendents maintain the "I want to be alone" or closed door policy and can be reached only after countless memos, surveys, and conferences with assistant superintendents. Once all the "bugs" have been removed from a particular procedure or plan, an appointment is made with the superintendent, and the library supervisor is allowed to present the written plan or procedure (having been coached first in the precise manner of doing this by some other member of the hierarchy.) One will find, however, that the closed door superintendent has a standard method of dealing with requests: he wants more data! No matter how completely one may feel that figures have been compiled, or how copious the written plan may be, or how many endorsements the plan may carry, this superintendent is an absolute genius at discovering some type of information, no matter how small, that has been omitted. His decision on the matter is then taken under advisement until such time as the additional data is gathered. Then, of course, he discovers another bit of data that has been overlooked. There is, however, one advantage to this data gathering process. Over the period of time and number of meetings that this takes, the superintendent and the library supervisor begin to get acquainted, and if the supervisor is skilled in human relationships, competent in knowledge, and determined in her goals, mutual respect grows and agreement can be reached.

Model Two: The *"Let's Get Everybody Involved" Superintendent*
A more difficult type of superintendent to work with is the "let's get everybody involved" administrator. By involving "everyone" in the smallest decision, the superintendent can easily find a number of scapegoats for plans that go awry. One library supervisor (having no budget with which to work) approached the superintendent in the hall one day with the simple question, "Do you suppose there would be any district funds available for the printing of Christmas bibliographies to be given to our elementary children?" The superintendent indicated that this was a splendid idea and immediately invited her into his office for a chat. As the interview progressed, he suggested that she:

Life with School Administrators

1. Hold a contest among high school art students for the cover design of the bibliographies.
2. Survey printing companies for quotes on printing costs.
3. Bring back samples of stock on which the bibliographies and covers are to be printed.
4. Call a meeting of district art teachers and representative principals to decide on color, style, etc. of the finished product.
5. Initiate a "favorite Christmas book" contest in each elementary school and appoint a committee of teacher-judges from each school to determine the winning reviews to appear in the bibliography.
6. Develop a committee of patrons to add "parent's choices" to the bibliography.
7. Prepare publicity releases and submit them to the publicity committee and the school public relations' office for approval.
8. Arrange for actual printing and distribution of bibliographies.
9. Arrange for a news photographer from each local paper to get a picture of the children receiving the bibliographies.

One can imagine what happens in this same office when a *major* decision has to be made!

Agreeing on Basic Goals

The administrative structure of the school district, then, determines the direction the library supervisor must take to get the program moving. It is usually more advantageous to present initial plans for the program to the director of elementary curriculum and, with his help and approval, begin cautious overtures to each of the administrators involved.

While it has already been pointed out that one is working not with ten or fifteen schools but with the individuals who make up the administration and staff of those schools, a word of caution is necessary. *Uniformity* is essential in any district-wide program so far as it is feasible to make the program uniform in each school. Early goals should not be overwhelming and agreement can generally be obtained (with effort) on the following:

1. The _____ School District plans to establish initial collections of library materials in every school where space for such a collection exists.
2. Materials for the initial collection will come from teachers *who wish to donate* room library materials to the centralized collection, and from federal and district funds which will henceforth be used in building these collections.
3. Because of the number of schools and the lack of trained librarians for each school, principals will recommend volunteers from among the patrons of their school to work with the library supervisor in establishing collections. The supervisor will provide a manual for volunteer use in carrying out processing and organization of materials.
4. New materials to be added to collections will be selected by the supervisor on the basis of curriculum need and requests of teachers and students.
5. Collections of materials will be organized (classified and cataloged) and prepared for circulation. Circulation policies will be developed and will be uniform throughout the district.
6. Standard school furniture used initially in elementary libraries will be replaced as funds permit with library furnishings suitable for elementary children.

It should be noted that each of these early goals deals with the physical aspects of establishing initial library collections. In those schools where the principal is audiovisually minded (and audiovisual materials exist), collections of nonprint materials should be established concurrently with print collections. In schools where few audiovisual materials are found, print collections will, of necessity, be established first. The ultimate goal, of course, is the establishment of media centers in every school and as funds become available, print and nonprint collections will be built simultaneously.

Educational Goals

While the implementation of physical goals can proceed on a rather straight course, the educational goals of the media center take far longer to implement. It is true that most educators would be in agreement with the goals of the materials center, but lip service and actual practice are two different things.

Media Center Goals

Verbally Stated	Actual Practice
Students should become independent in their pursuit of knowledge.	Classroom instruction is group oriented.
Students should have access to a wide variety of carriers of knowledge.	The major learning vehicle utilized in most schools is the basic text.
Students should be helped to acquire skills of location, acquisition, integration, organization, recording, and evaluation of knowledge through *functional activities*.	Students become well acquainted with the prepared worksheet.
Students should not merely have the ability to read but should develop a love of reading and discover the enjoyment that can come from books.	Ample time allotted for reading instruction rarely includes time for pleasure reading.
Students should become visually literate and adept at securing information from nonprint sources as well as print sources.	In many schools only teachers are allowed to handle audiovisual materials.

Obtaining agreement on these goals by all those involved is relatively easy, but implementing them is another matter altogether and requires patience, fortitude and supersalesmanship.

The Supervisor as a Super Salesman

An earlier reference to Willie Loman, while perhaps made partly in jest, carried with it serious overtones. The stereotyped image of the school librarian is accepted by far too many eduators and reenforced by many librarians themselves. Thus the competent supervisor, who must at times be forceful and always display energy and enthusiasm, comes as a shock to those who have had little experience with this new breed of educator.

The key to establishing and developing an effective elementary instructional materials center program lies with the library/media supervisor. She must know what she is doing; she must be determined to see the job through; she must be able to sell the program to everyone she meets who might have the slightest interest in children and learning. No individual is too unimportant to be sold, and no opportunity is too slight to be taken advantage of. The supervisor's enthusiasm, like gamma rays, penetrates the area which surrounds her. By the end of a typical day she may be:

> Bent like a corkscrew from carrying boxes;
>
> Have blisters on her feet from performing the hundred mile dash out of one building and into another;
>
> Have broken every fingernail to the quick from opening cartons that were never meant to be opened;

and yet, as she applies vaseline to the burns received from using an overhot electric stylus, she smiles, (sometimes through clenched teeth) but she smiles for any audience present and leaves the impression that no sacrifice is too great to bring this great and glorious materials center into being.

In salesmanship, enthusiasm is the key and should be conveyed not only through the overall attitude of the supervisor, but in all oral and written communication. For it is an axiom that principals (more or less) do have control over their faculties;

and that teachers (more or less) have complete control over the where-abouts of their students—though this last point is debated by some. Therefore, if teachers and principals are not convinced of the value of this new addition to the school called an instructional materials center, the only time the students will see the center is via a quick glance in the door while passing on their way to some other class.

Written communication to administrators and faculty members is generally one of four types:
(1) the "pat on the back" approach, (2) the "cry in the night" approach, (3) the "blow one's own horn" approach, and (4) the "let's get moving" approach. Examples of each of these follow:

1. *The "pat on the back" approach*

The old maxim that one can catch more flies with sugar than with vinegar applies equally to the supervisor who can make more converts to the library program with a pat on the back than she can with criticism.

This generally takes the form of a district-wide library/media newsletter. The newsletter usually contains items such as new materials acquired for use by students and teachers in a particular school (in the hope that the "have nots" will pressure their administrator into acquiring the same materials for them) and successful activities undertaken by specific classes utilizing the facilities of the center. This latter pat on the back serves as an extrinsic reward to both teachers and students who like to see their activities in print and will often generate more projects in the hope that these too will be sufficiently newsworthy to be broadcast throughout the district through the newsletter.

2. *The "cry in the night" approach*

Faced in many cases with the overwhelming task of building something from nothing, the library supervisor can easily become discouraged early in the game. While grieving quietly may bring some comfort to the bereaved, it will not be in the least effective in improving the situation. Therefore, it is essential that the supervisor in loud, clear and certain terms, make the basic needs of the program known to those who can do something about it. Thus, the "cry in the night" approach should actually be a "howl in the night."

The new library supervisor, who generally finds herself at the outset of the program without adequate budget or staff can overdo this approach. But if it is true that the wheel that squeaks the loudest gets the oil, it is also true that she has the squeakiest wheel in the school district. While the "cry in the night" is usually in the form of a memo to the administrator who has the power of the budget or other necessary item, the memo must in some way be creatively done, lest it become lost in the stack of other memos on the administrator's desk from supervisors in art, music, remedial reading, band, speech, math, science, social studies, language arts, kindergarten, and physical education. Memos should be short and to the point. Two examples are illustrated.

EXAMPLE ONE: The Plea for Space

    To: Administrator A
    From: The Elementary Library Supervisor
    Subject: SPACE   SPACE   SPACE   SPACE   SPACE

We cannot:

1. Introduce materials for units of work.
2. Teach vitally necessary research skills.
3. Develop a love of reading through book talks and individual pupil guidance.
4. Supervise and guide students in individual and class research.
5. Confer with teachers and meet teacher and pupil demands.
6. Maintain a well organized and easily accessible collection of materials.
7. Supervise listening and viewing activities.

    In: Cafeterias
         Hallways
         Closets

Life with School Administrators 23

We must have:
A minimum of two full classrooms of space, centrally located.

(ALA Standards recommend 40 square feet per student based on 25 percent of the school's enrollment)

EXAMPLE TWO: The Plea for Staff

To: Administrator A
From: Your Good Friend, the Library Supervisor
Subject: 15 Basket Cases Who Need Help!

Elementary librarians are carrying full responsibility for complete library service in two schools. They are required to schedule classes for work/study skill sessions, introduce materials for units of work in the classroom (please note that 66 units are going on in any one school at any given time), as well as give full service in reading guidance and research and reference activities based on FULL TIME DEMAND while having less than full time in each building. In addition, each librarian is circulating between 30,000 and 55,000 items per building per year.

WE NEED HELP !!!!

I respectfully request a meeting with you to discuss the possibility of presenting to the Board of Education a comprehensive plan for the addition of _____ professional librarians and supportive staff for the _____ school year.

3. The "Blow One's Own Horn" Approach

Accountability may be a somewhat new concept on the educational scene today and has been praised by those in higher education as a long overdue part of the educational process. It is not, however, a new concept to school administrators. When the supervisor makes a plea for a budget of ten dollars per child for the coming year, her superior immediately wants to know how wisely the fifty cents allocated per child for library materials the previous year was spent. And woe to the supervisor who does not have this information at her fingertips. The best way to avoid being caught in the central office hallway by an administrator who wants some immediate information is to keep the information constantly flowing to his desk. Tell him daily, if necessary, what an excellent job you and other members of the library staff are doing. Lose no opportunity to prove your worth, (statistically, if possible). Administrators are less likely to argue with accurate statistics than with assumptions or subjective evaluations.

One supervisor, hearing by the grapevine that the Board of Education was demanding an austerity budget for the coming year, including cuts in staff, did not wait to act until the rumor became reality. Strange as it may seem, it is not the worth of a particular educational program that determines its continued existence within a district, but the longevity of the program. Since elementary library/media programs are generally the newest to be added, without a well-thought-out battle plan on the part of the supervisor, they may be the first to get the ax when cuts are contemplated.

Even in the face of false rumors, or without the threat of an austerity budget, it behooves the library supervisor to keep the worth of the program continually in front of administrative eyes and ears. One week before the proposed staff cuts were made public by the district, our aforementioned supervisor sent the following memo to every administrator in the district.

> To: All District Administrators
> From: The Library Supervisor
> Subject: Evaluation of Elementary IMC Goals
>
> *Rationale for Evaluation*
> The major emphasis of the elementary library/media program since its inception has been the development of work/study skills on the part of students for the independent location, acquisition, organization, recording, and evaluation of information. Our major concern has been and will continue to be helping students to learn how to learn in order that they may know success in a world where, (research indicates) the total knowledge of mankind doubles

Life with School Administrators 25

every generation. In 1970 the district average for students in grades K through 9 was the 25th percentile on the Iowa Test of Basic Skills. By 1974 this average had risen to the 75th percentile. An independent evaluation of the resource centers' program by _____ University in 1974 concluded that "In the area of skills development, considerable progress has been made with students being able to demonstrate needed skills for independent research projects. The results of this program now in its fourth year are statistically significant."

_____ University's evaluation is supported by the current results of this year's testing program which are as follows:

Actual Grade Level	Expected Level of Achievement	Actual Achievement
3.0	4.0	4.5
4.0	5.0	5.8
5.0	6.0	7.1
6.0	7.0	8.6
7.0	8.0	9.7
8.0	9.0	10.8
9.0	10.0	11.5

Conclusions of this year's testing program:
1. District students are making an eleven and one-half year gain in nine years of education in development of independent study skills.
2. Students at every grade level are scoring above their expected achievement level.

FOR NEXT YEAR
The library staff will continue to develop and to adapt materials and programs suited to our students' specific needs in order to maintain and improve the high level of quality in the work/study skills program. It is also our desire to develop a program of reading guidance comparable in quality to the work/study skills program. However, this new program will not be possible until full staffing of the resource centers becomes a reality.

We are most appreciative of the cooperation and support of the administration for the program and hope that you will feel that the above results indicate that the program has been worthy of your support.
(No cuts were made in the library staff.)

4. *The "let's get moving" approach*

A visit to many school library/media centers might reveal some surprising facts. In schools where such centers have been established, and more often in schools where such centers are not staffed by professional personnel, the centers are frequently empty, or perhaps used for study halls. Students who do visit the centers seem to do so with little direction or purpose. Teachers are not aware of the contents of the library, and materials which should be in frequent use are gathering dust on the shelves.

One of the sad facts of life in the library/media field is that in many schools not only are media services unused, but only the library/media personnel seem to be aware of the absolutely indispensable value of their services. Life in the media center moves along with an occasional visitor or teacher who drops by at coffee break time with some inane remark like "Isn't this nice that we have this beautiful library in our school!" But the same teacher, if the suggestion is made that she might consider turning her students loose in the center to learn, reacts like a mother tigress whose cubs are threatened by imminent disaster. The defensive mechanism immediately goes up and like a standard recording, the words pour out: "Oh, no! We don't have time for extras. I'm too busy teaching basic skills. The children wouldn't behave and I wouldn't want to bother you!"

Therefore, the more subtle approach is taken. Memos to teachers listing the services of the media center staff sometimes help (along with a willingness to perform these services). But a more positive way to get teachers moving is to waylay any students who get near the center and entice them in. Show them all of the "goodies" available for their use. Build their enthusiasm concerning activities they might pursue in the center. Then *burst* the balloon by stating, "Of course, you will need your teacher's

Life with School Administrators 27

permission to make slides, or view filmstrips or whatever—just bring me an okay from your teacher and we will get started!" If the teacher wants any peace the rest of the school year, she might begin turning her students loose. Once the librarian has access to the students, then a subtle approach to the teacher concerning the relevance of their IMC activities to classroom studies can follow as will the eventual integration of classroom/media center activities.

In summary then, the new library supervisor is faced with eleven basic tasks. She must:

1. Survey the schools.
2. Establish rapport with the administration.
3. Write recommendations.
4. Collect and order materials.
5. Find space.
6. Develop a volunteer manual.
7. Establish working volunteer groups.
8. Initiate the battle for professional and clerical help.
9. Supervise the physical processing of materials.
10. Prepare to open for business.
11. Develop and implement an on-going sales campaign for effective library/media center use.

With careful nurturing, library/media programs do have a way of achieving spectacular growth in a short period of time. Lest the supervisor feel her work is finished when the above steps have been taken, this growth in materials, space, staff, programs and services creates a unique set of problems all its own. Such problems involve working with volunteers and professional staff members, federal programs, budgets, salesmen, computers and a host of other jolly things. Now that you have passed "go" in the world of the library supervisor, for more fun and games, you may move to chapter two.

2
The Vodka in the Punch— or Never Entertain a Volunteer

Elementary materials centers' programs abound with volunteers. Few school administrators would consider placing a volunteer in charge of a high school library, but working on the misguided "anybody can teach first grade" philosophy, district elementary library/media programs are often started with volunteers who can, with guidance, be most helpful, but turned loose on their own can only create a Frankenstein monster over which the professional librarian may never gain control. This unhappy situation occurs through a combination of circumstances. Many school administrators emerge to a supervisory post by way of a secondary physical education background. It is assumed that around the age of forty or so when the coach's demonstrations turn into explanations, said coach decides that twenty years in a school district ought to entitle him to something better than sweaty locker rooms. Thus he goes back to the ivy halls for a few courses in administration (or pulls out the administrator's certificate earned in 1950 he has been saving for retirement) and becomes a principal or superintendent.

This background augers problems for the elementary schools. While the administrator may have some understanding of the purpose of the elementary school (since he once attended this institution himself), he has little or no understanding of the purposes of the elementary library/media center, for this facility did not exist during the time he was dipping pigtails in inkwells.

Never Entertain a Volunteer

One outcome of this lack of understanding is the broom closet collection of tattered and worn books, organized and administered by the volunteer mothers from the patrons' or mothers' club of the school. The new library supervisor encountering this "library" for the first time should be prepared for one or more of the following:

The Materials Collection: Volunteer Style
1. In the initial collection, all books are taped by reading level and/or subject matter. Reading level generally is determined by the size of the book rather than the contents. Thus, Pearl Buck's *The Big Wave* is given a red tape and placed with the easy readers since it happens to be a small book. (Everyone knows, of course, that all small books are easy to read.) Carolyn Haywood's *Betsy's Little Star* receives a blue tape and finds its way to the upper grade shelf (being a larger book than *The Big Wave*.)
2. Size, rather than interest determines the particular book a child may choose. The second grader may want dinosaurs (which resides on the forbidden upper grade shelf) but must settle for *Dick and Jane Go to School*. After all, we wouldn't want a child to take a book he couldn't read, would we?
3. In more advanced collections, color taping may indicate the subject of the book. The subject of course is determined by the title. *The Cat and Mrs. Cary* receives a green tape indicating that it belongs with the pet books, and *The Pushcart War* gets a pink tape to show that it belongs on the history shelf.
4. Some volunteers having visited the public library have noted that some books carry numbers on the spine. By obtaining someone's cast-off sixth edition of Dewey, these enterprising volunteers proceed to classify the collection. Dewey proving somewhat confusing, on first glance, the mothers decide that any number giving a general idea of the subject of the book will suffice. All books remotely connected with science receive a 500. All books mentioning other lands or historical events (again determined by title) receive a 900, etc. While this system does not carry too much advantage over the color tape system, it does, at least, look more "official."

5. Students may select one book they may keep for one week (providing the volunteer's son does not come down with the measles on library day; in that event, they keep the book for two weeks or for the duration of the bout of measles.)

6. Student visits are restricted to this weekly book selection activity. A student who might attempt to seek information in this somewhat unorthodox collection of materials is discouraged either by his teacher who "doesn't want the nice volunteers to be bothered" or by the collection itself, a researcher's nightmare.

Enter the New Library Supervisor

The unsuspecting supervisor who walks into the "library already established by volunteers" situation generally finds less than overwhelming enthusiasm for the program on the part of students and teachers. But the slightest flicker of an eye which might indicate some degree of dismay is absolutely forbidden. Along with teeth-clenching mentioned earlier, tongue-biting is also a recommended talent for every library supervisor. One major reason for praising the "really great job" done by the volunteers is *money*.

A school district cannot operate too well without funds. These funds are acquired in the form of taxes which come for the most part from local taxpayers. Volunteer mothers *are* local taxpayers! Therefore:

Criticism	equals	One Unhappy Mother
One Unhappy Mother	equals	More Unhappy Mothers
More Unhappy Mothers	equal	Refusal to Work for (or vote for) the local tax levy for the school
No tax levy	equals	No School!

Moral to be noted by the library supervisor:

KEEP YOUR MOUTH CLOSED, DEAR!

In this situation the supervisor has no choice but to work with the volunteers and as tactfully as possibly, make suggestions for improvement. Dramatic improvement within a short time is not to be expected. It is also possible that the supervisor may not be able to walk on eggs for any considerable length of time without breaking one or two. But tactful suggestions for improvement combined with copious amounts of praise can bring change.

The reader may by now have the impression that library supervisors do not welcome the assistance of volunteer aides. This is far from the truth. Since the initial establishment of elementary library services by volunteers has been the exception rather than the rule in the nation's schools, the foregoing situation will not be met too often. It is mentioned since the possibility of encountering such a situation does exist. It is more likely, however, that the new supervisor will be charged with the complete responsibility for establishing library/media centers in the schools for the first time. It is also very likely that inadequate professional or clerical help will be available. The only way, then, that materials centers will be established is to recruit and train volunteers. With cautious selection and careful training, volunteer aides can be a boon to any library/media program.

Where Do They Come From?

Volunteer library aides are nearly always the mothers of the students in the school. They may serve in this capacity to get away from home once a week, to keep a closer eye on their child, to find out what the neighbor's children are doing in school, or simply because they enjoy the work. They are obtained by two methods:

1. A general call for help put out by the principal:
   At PTA meetings   or
   Mother's Club Meetings   or
   By a letter which goes home with every child   or
   By a telephone survey of the school's patrons

2. Through teacher-principal recommendation of specific mothers who are known *not* to be:
   opinionated
   nosey

uncooperative
talkative

This second method is by far the best, for a good volunteer can be the librarian's right hand, while those with the negative qualities listed can make life hell on earth (or in the school as the case may be). Note the earlier references to Dante! Even with the most careful selection, certain basic types of less desirable volunteers may occasionally appear on the scene and must be worked with one way or another. One type who is more a bother than a problem is the "community leader" who, hearing of the new project in the school, volunteers to help. She will be on hand for the first training session or two (long enough to get her picture in the paper) but quickly loses interest when faced with the reality of hundreds or thousands of books that need sorting, classifying, cataloging, and processing. Some mothers find the more mundane aspects of preparing for the opening of a materials center are compensated by the social aspects of the work. While these mothers enjoy getting away from home once or twice a week, even for the less than exciting activity of pasting pockets in books, the community leader must soon seek what she feels are more creative outlets for her talents.

A more difficult type of volunteer with whom the supervisor must sometimes deal is the overly capable, "damn the torpedoes, full speed ahead" type of gal. This dear lady takes the bulldozer approach to the preparation of materials. (It should be noted here that no matter how carefully directions may have been prepared, or regardless of the amount of training given to volunteers, problems and questions will arise.) Assuming that our harried supervisor is attempting to oversee the activities of more than one group of volunteers in more than one school at a time, it follows that when she is in one school she cannot be in another. The absence or presence of the supervisor does not in the least bother Mrs. Gung Ho. She forges right ahead with the work, moving into areas which may not have been covered in training and inventing her own systems as she goes. If a book does not look "important" to her, she may decide catalog cards aren't necessary, for she can't imagine any purpose for which someone might want it. Duplicate titles may all receive the same accession number since they are identical books. These and a host of original other ideas can make the process of information retrieval challenging to say the least (or frustrating, if you prefer), and require constant vigilance on the part of the supervisor.

Finally, in the school where the privacy of the teachers' lounge is not as enforced as it should be, we have the mother who likes to keep the pot boiling and spends as much time in the lounge as she does in the library. Since this is a place where teachers generally vent their frustrations (providing a happier alternative than venting them on the children), this pair of uninvited ears can prove disastrous. Granted, teachers generally control themselves when mother-helpers are around, however, the "pot-boiler" has been known to stand outside the door of the lounge taking in such comments as that of Miss D, a third grade teacher, who on a particularly trying day, was heard to say, "God damn, someday I'm going to invent a magic wand, wave it over those kids, turn them all into mosquitoes, and go SLAP, SPLAT, SQUASH!" This same teacher could do little but stare blankly at the principal the next day when called in for a conference and told that he had received reports that she considered her students less than insects and had a deep urge for their destruction! Fortunately, the teacher got to the source of the report and was not left to wonder what fellow teacher took her fantasy seriously. The teachers' lounge continues to be a place for letting off steam with one addition—guard duty to prevent unseen mothers is now a must!

Even the supervisor is not immune to the administrative fire drills caused by the "deeply concerned" or overly dedicated volunteer. One supervisor working alone one day checking in new materials for the library/media center in a first year school was approached by a mother with whom she had worked in another school the previous year. The mother had proved herself to be an efficient and hardworking volunteer, amiable and at the same time truly concerned about the education of her children. With the opening of the new school and the redrawing of attendance areas the mother was justifiably concerned that her children would have the excellent facilities in the new school that they had had in the previous school. By the time her tour of inspection brought her to the library, she found the supervisor with cartons of books on the floor surrounded by section upon section of empty shelves. Doing a bit of quick mathematics, the mother determined that six cartons of books would not fill twenty-four sections of thirty-six by seventy-two inch shelving. She asked the supervisor to expound on specific needs for the new library/media center.

The unthinking supervisor, glancing around at all of the empty space, replied, "We need everything." She did add that "in any brand new school there are many needs" but the damage had been done. That same night, this well-meaning mother contacted a member of the District's Board of Education, the Superintendent of Schools, the Principal of this particular school, and countless other parents to make them aware of the necessity for providing instructional materials for the children. The source of her information concerning the inadequacy of resource center materials she attributed to the *library supervisor.*

The result of this well-meaning complaint was a traumatic conference between the library supervisor on the one hand and the combined wrath of the superintendent, the principal, the assistant superintendent, and the Board member on the other. While the cause of the mother's comments was easily determined, the misinformation dispensed to many persons was difficult to counteract. In an effort to smooth the troubled waters, the Supervisor did appear as a speaker at the next parents' meeting to discuss the library program and to answer questions. In addition, in the interval preceeding the meeting, new materials which arrived were quickly processed and shelved, giving the resource center (which was on display for the meeting) a more respectable appearance than previously.

Training the Library-Media Volunteer

The training program for volunteers has two distinct phases. Volunteers can be most helpful in setting up an initial collection of materials, if they are carefully selected and well trained in the numerous processes necessary for the job. In addition, volunteers will probably be needed initially (until such time as adequate professional staff is available) for keeping the library/media centers in operation once they have been opened. The natural tendency on the part of the supervisor is to get the required number of volunteers working as quickly as possible and to rush the process along. Pressure from both administrators and teachers to get the center in operation can be great. Teachers see cartons of materials delivered to the school, and if the work area is unfortunately located near a main hallway, they will frequently stop to browse, leaving the impression with volunteers that it is a shame that these beautiful new materials are being held up for processing when the children in the school ought to be enjoying them. The effect of this sometimes not so subtle pressure is the tendency on the part of the volunteers to want to cut corners to get the job done quickly, or the development of a martyr complex (i.e. "no matter how much we do, someone always wants more.")

In order to avoid the countless problems that will arise from sloppy or careless processing of materials, the supervisor must take as much time as is required with volunteers to be sure that they have a thorough understanding of what is to be done and how it is to be done, and most importantly, *why* a particular process is important. For this purpose, a manual should be developed, giving in detail the steps necessary for preparing materials for the school library. The manual should be clear and free of jargon and technical terminology. At the risk of offending catalogers everywhere, supervisors discover that mothers can relate to the term "author card" but not to "main entry." Books are "checked out" to students rather than "charged." Books are placed on the shelves rather than in the stacks. While these and a host of other simplified terms may approach heresy in the opinion of many librarians, the supervisor finds that when faced with the problem of technical semantics or getting the job done with some understanding, the latter course takes priority.

Simplifying the Processing Task
In working with untrained volunteers in the initial processing

of materials for the library, it is prudent to review the steps required and to simplify as many of these steps as possible and still enable the student to go through the process of information retrieval as nontraumaticly as possible. Faced in many instances with hundreds of books and audiovisual items donated from classrooms for which printed cards are not available, the supervisor has two choices:

1. Do full cataloging for each item, setting a target date for the opening of the new library about five years hence.
2. Perform only those processes absolutely necessary to provide for the efficient location and acquisition of information contained in each item.

The question of what is considered "absolutely necessary" in the preparation of materials for the library is one that has been debated by librarians since the beginning of time (or libraries, whichever came first). The amount of time put into materials preparation will depend on the use to which the library/media center is to be put, and the philosophy of the supervisor concerning those processes considered essential.

Large and Small Group Training
Volunteer training generally takes two forms:

1. Multi-session training meetings on district-wide level for explanation of the philosophy, goals and objectives of the program.
2. On the job, in-service training of small volunteer groups within individual schools in the district.

Since basic philosophy and policies concerning the operation and effective utilization of the materials center should have been developed before the recruitment of volunteers takes place, the initial training session, whether in large or small groups, should cover these policies. If, for example, mothers understand that uniformity of subject headings is important if students are to locate all the material that is needed on a subject, they will not be so prone to dream up and assign their own subject headings while waiting for the librarian or supervisor to ride the weekly circuit back to their school. If it is explained that students expect to find nearly all materials on the same subject shelved together under the same Dewey number, again, they may hold off playing guessing games and assigning their own number should the librarian be delayed in her regularly scheduled visit to the school.

Volunteer training should include not only the whys and wherefores of processing, but careful, repeated checking on the part of the supervisor to be sure that all steps outlined in the manual are completely understood. This same careful checking should continue once a center has opened to assure consistency and uniformity in organization and operation. Supervisors who have worked with volunteers for any length of time know that without clear, written directions and constant checking, the following errors are extremely common:

1. If books are taped, Volunteer A places the tape one inch from the bottom of the spine while Volunteer B places it two inches from the bottom. Volunteer C uses the gummed tapes which come with the processing kits with no additional fortification and by the following morning they have fallen off the books and on to the floor.

2. If accession numbers are used, the volunteer will frequently jump from a 99 number to the next thousand. For example, 1298, 1299, 2000.

3. Volunteer A places the pockets in the front of the book, volunteer B places them in the back.

4. Volunteer C is glue happy. She squirts glue on book pockets as if she were decorating a cake. As she slaps the book shut, the glue spreads beyond the pocket, and flyleaf and back cover are glued solidly together.

5. Volunteer D is a "butterfingers." She drops cards ready to file, she knocks right and left books which have been sorted for marking and generally creates chaos.

These and a host of other approaches to processing can take valuable time to correct in the years that follow. Thus, uniformity and consistency are a must in any activity directed by the supervisor and performed by volunteers.

In addition to the preparation of a manual for processing materials for the library/media center, written procedures should be developed for the uniform administration of the program once the center is open and in use. If the continued use of volunteers is necessary to maintain library operations and to perform the daily routines necessary in any school's materials center, again uniformity and consistency are essential. Every staff member as well as the volunteers should have a copy of the operational policies of the center. Such policies should be carefully explained to students in order that materials may be easily accessible to all who need them and the borrowing and use of materials can take place with as little confusion and red tape as possible.

Written material prepared by the supervisor for volunteer use should, then, include the following:

1. A statement of the library/media center's philosophy, goals, and policies
2. Careful, detailed instructions for the preparation of materials for the center
3. Careful, detailed instructions for the operation of the center.

Scheduling of Volunteers

In order that the preparations for opening a center can move in an orderly fashion, and that once centers have opened they will be fully staffed, the scheduling of volunteer aides is a necessity. The best method of scheduling is to turn this responsibility over to a willing volunteer who will see that all scheduled work periods are adequately covered and that substitutes are obtained when needed. The advantages of allowing a volunteer handle the scheduling (aside from the obvious advantage of relieving the supervisor of part of the workload) are found in better public relations for the school district. It is not too disastrous if a volunteer allows a slight hint of exasperation to appear in her voice when told for the fourth week in a row by the same volunteer that she cannot work on a particular day. It would be fatal if the library supervisor showed the slightest hint of displeasure with a volunteer. Nor would hurt feelings be as prevalent if a mother were told by a volunteer that her services were not needed on a particular day (since ten other mothers have indicated that that is the *only* day they can work) than if the library supervisor turned down an offer of help. Even with volunteers, the saturation point can be reached!

This brings us to one last but important point in working with volunteers. They must be kept busy! Too many volunteers scheduled to work at the same time will result in someone not having enough to do, and a bored volunteer is an ex-volunteer. In summary, the following principles should be kept in mind when recruiting and working with volunteers:

1. Develop a written philosophy and statement of goals and policies.
2. Select volunteers carefully. Rely on teacher-principal recommendation.
3. Hold an initial meeting of all volunteers to explain philosophy, policy, goals, and activities.
4. Prepare and introduce the volunteer manual. Wording in the manual should be simple but procedures should be detailed.
5. Work with the volunteers on procedures until they are well understood.
6. Be available to answer questions and untangle snags.
7. Arrange for scheduling of volunteer activities.
8. Avoid criticism. Make suggestions tactfully. Be appreciative.
9. Keep each volunteer busy in a job suited to her talents.
10. Provide some type of reward for a job well done.

Speaking of Rewards: The Vodka in the Punch

The best laid plans of mice and men (and library supervisors) can, and often do, go awry. Little did one library supervisor realize that after threading her way cautiously and successfully through the first nine steps listed above, that step ten could be her downfall! The year had been a fruitful one. Agreement had been achieved on policies and goals. Volunteers performed their tasks faithfully and eleven materials centers were made ready in one year's time for their grand openings. The sore backs, broken nails, glue to be cleaned off of clothes, burned fingers, and other joys encountered in the hundreds of volunteer hours spent could not go unrewarded. Several forms of reward were considered ranging from printed certificates to gifts, and the decision was made to hold a library tea to provide the opportunity for Board Members and top administrators to personally thank the mothers for a job well done.

The scene of this gala affair was to be a middle school auditorium. Invited guests, in addition to the volunteers, included the Mayor of the town, a State Senator (both up for reelection in the fall), a children's author, and a noted illustrator.

Preparations for the tea went forth without a hitch. Printed invitations were issued; mothers baked hundreds of cookies; teachers donated their coffee and tea services, punch bowls and linen table cloths; the school nurse prepared a special flower arrangement to serve as a centerpiece on the tea table; and just before the arrival of the guests, the mother's club president brought in her specially made punch. This fine Christian lady volunteered her afternoon to remain by the punch bowl to supervise the student helpers who were to serve. (The helpers, incidentally, were ten- and eleven-year old girls.)

The fatal error was made when the supervising mother left the tea table for one reason or another (the student helpers not having arrived as yet), and the PE instructor on an earlier dare from the faculty, proceeded to spike the punch. The lovely punch bowl became the proud possessor of two pints of vodka purchased especially for the occasion! The library supervisor noted all of this activity from the door where she was greeting arriving guests, with the thought going through her mind that the gentlemen in the crowd might enjoy the afternoon's activities a bit more than they had anticipated—but otherwise, not too concerned.

The guests arrived and the activities got underway. What was to have been a short "welcome and thank you" affair passed the two-hour mark of speeches as the Mayor and the Senator extolled their accomplishments to their captive audience under the painful smiles of the author and the illustrator. These dear ladies, when finally given the floor, cut their talks quite short (being most sympathetic to mothers who had to beat their kids home from school.) Thus, while the mothers scurried home the minute the speeches were ended, the gentlemen gathered around the punch bowl for a short time, but even they could not lower the level significantly (which is usually the case when three or four people are trying to make a dent in refreshments prepared for fifty).

As the supervisor was bidding the last of the guests goodbye, she heard the startled voice of the custodian saying, "OH, MY GOD, LOOK AT THEM KIDS DRINKING THAT PUNCH. THEY'LL GO HOME DRUNK AS SKUNKS!" The student helpers were, indeed, cheerfully downing the booze. While not quite able to leap a building with a single bound, the supervisor took three tables in one jump, grabbed up the punch bowl under the startled eyes of the supervising mother, proceeded to the kitchen and emptied the contents in the sink! It was a choice of telling the mother what had happened to her lovely punch recipe or allowing the dear lady to think that the library supervisor had gone mad from overwork. The latter choice was made.

By the time the children were bundled off home, the supervisor debated the wisdom of informing the powers-that-be of a rather peculiar set of circumstances which might lead a group of little girls to go reeling in the doors of their homes that evening. She decided to stay with the tried and true, three-pronged approach to most problems in the library/media field (i.e. grit the teeth, smile, and keep your mouth closed, dear). Fortunately, any strange behavior on the part of the children must have been attributed to the heat or growing pains as no administrator's phone rang that night!

As one can see, life with volunteers can be tons of fun. But the time must come, if the elementary library/media program is to prove its worth, for a professional staff to take over. Having come this far along in the game of library supervisor, the reader is now ready to experience the joys and headaches of supervising the activities of the professional staff.

Titles Mentioned in this Chapter
Haywood, Carolyn. *Betsy's Little Star*. Morrow, 1950
Gates, Doris. *The Cat and Mrs. Cary*. Viking, 1962
Merrill, Jean. *The Pushcart War*. Young Scott Books, 1964

3

Eureka! A Staff of Twelve

Library supervisors and school administrators live in two different worlds. What is reality to the supervisor is fantasy to the administrator. Once the supervisor has managed to establish the nucleus of a materials collection in each school in a district, the administrator sees the program as an established reality and considers the major portion of the supervisor's job finished. The supervisor knows that the job has just begun. Assuming that she has made it to the "center established in each school" phase, with little or no professional or clerical help, and inadequate budget, space, and materials, she can either throw in the towel, or hitch up her girdle and prepare to launch the major battle of the campaign—the battle for staff.

Before launching such a battle she picks up her copy of *Pippi Longstocking* and reviews the chapter where Pippi (with ease) conquers two policemen singlehandedly, and perhaps, reaches for her Bible, not for prayer, but to review David's tactics in conquering Goliath. Thus armed with these inspirational passages, she goes forth to the administrative battleground.

The need for professional staff members may be so obvious to the library supervisor, that unless she is prepared for the general attitudes that prevail concerning the elementary library/media center, and has some understanding of the reason for such attitudes, sheer exasperation may defeat her cause before she gets the campaign off the ground. Fact number one that must be faced is that most administrators do not see the need for professional personnel at the elementary level.

In launching the campaign for additional professional and clerical staff, the supervisor must be aware of the myths to which many traditional administrators and teachers cling concerning the elementary materials centers. For example, in the State of Missouri, one must assume that the State Department of Education feels that less professional help is needed by elementary than secondary students since the librarian/pupil ratio requirement is higher for elementary than for secondary schools (1500/1 elementary; 1200/1 secondary). Therefore, if permanent gains are to be made, the battle lines must be drawn on two fronts. The first campaign is undertaken in the school district, but a second front must be established through state librarians' organizations which can pressure state department personnel to strengthen requirements. Some of the myths concerning elementary instructional materials centers were discussed in chapter one. Others which the supervisor will meet are as follows:

Myth
Teachers know what they want to teach and how they want to teach. A good teacher needs nothing more than a textbook and a blackboard.

Reality
In this age of the information explosion, the greatest service we can provide our students is teaching them how to learn. Teachers as a whole are not proficient in the use of a wide variety of carriers of knowledge.

Myth
No money is available for additional staffing.

Reality
Money is available in school districts for cooks, bus drivers, swimming coaches, drama coaches, etc. How important is "learning how to learn"?

Myth
There is no space available for the kind of library in which

Reality
Space has been provided (in addition to classroom space)

Eureka! A Staff of Twelve 45

you would put a REAL librarian.

Myth
We need to spend money on materials before we can think about adding staff.

Myth
Volunteers have been very helpful in the program. We can continue to use them to run the libraries.

for eating and playing. Why can't space be provided for learning?

Reality
The most well-stocked materials center cannot become an educational force in the school unless teachers and students are trained in its use. This is the job of a professional library/media person.

Reality
Volunteers are helpful for performing routine tasks. They cannot stimulate teachers' thinking and develop creative learning activities. Nor can they implement the vitally necessary comprehensive program of work/study skill development.

One method of countering the myths is to make available to administrators studies which prove the effectiveness of a good library/media center program. While dated, a summary of research in the field is found in the May, 1962, *School Libraries*. This summary by Mary Gaver does point up the effectiveness of good school library programs. A more recent review of research in the field can be found in the summer and fall (1972) issues of *School Media Quarterly*. Here are found such a variety of studies on every phase of media programs that the supervisor should find helpful data to support her in her battle for staff. A number of the studies cited do point out the lack of teacher effectiveness in media center use without the guidance of trained, professional staff.

These studies, in all likelihood, will be supported by the librarian's own previous experience and statements based on practical experience can be helpful. The most useful studies to call upon are those which show a direct correlation between in-service training of teachers in library/media center use and increased academic achievement of students. Studies resulting from the Knapp Libraries project of the American Association of School Librarians are useful for this purpose. (See *Realization: The Final Report of the Knapp School Libraries Project,* edited by Peggy Sullivan and published by The American Library Association in 1968.)

The Year of the Memo

It is a mistake to rely solely on studies from other school districts in attempting to boost one's own program. While some studies may be helpful to prove a point, one must take care that administrators do not feel that *their* school district is being placed in an unfavorable light. It is particularly dangerous to compare progress made in one's own school district with that made in a neighboring school district. The reaction might well be an invitation to the supervisor to join some other school district if she does not feel that the program in which she is involved is the best in the area, or state, or country, or at whatever level the administrator uses for comparison. A better approach is to compare the present program in the district with what *everyone* in the district would like to see the program become. In a district which had one elementary librarian for every four schools (in accordance with State requirements) such a memo was developed and followed up with a meeting of the professional library staff with the Superintendent of Schools to clarify any points in the memo about which he might have questions.

TO: Superintendent of Schools
FROM: Elementary Librarians: (names listed here)
SUBJECT: *Improvement of the Elementary Materials Center Program*

Eureka! A Staff of Twelve

THE ELEMENTARY MATERIALS CENTER PROGRAM

What It Is

1. An aid to teachers and students in providing material to *supplement* the learning program.

2. A place where teachers and students get materials.

3. An opportunity for children to learn the joy of reading and to improve reading skills.

4. A source of help to teachers in unit work through introduction of materials to students for units of work on a *limited* basis.

5. In schools with limited space, a place where children get a book and leave.

What It Can Be

Second only to the teacher, the most vital educational force in the school; placing the emphasis on *learning*, rather than on teaching.

A tremendous motivational force through *helping children* select and use materials for maximum learning benefit.

A deliberate, all out effort to assure *each child* the selection of material appropriate to his reading level and suited to his interest.

A motivational resource for every teacher and every child taught, through close teacher-librarian planning of activities and materials to be used by children to create both the *desire* and opportunity to learn.

In schools where space permits, a vital force for the *independent* pursuit of knowledge through the use of a variety of materials, print and nonprint.

6. A program where work study skills needed by students throughout their lives are *taught*.

A program where work study skills for the independent pursuit of knowledge are *learned* through independent study activities of students under the helping hands of teachers and librarians.

How Elementary Librarians Spent Their Time Last Year

How Elementary Librarians Should Have Spent Their Time Last Year

Filing 42,945 catalog cards in the card catalog.

Assisting students with research problems.

Putting 259,010 book cards back in books returned by students.

In teacher/librarian conferences planning materials and activities for units of work.

Putting 259,010 books back in their proper place on the shelves.

Introducing materials for units of work to students to motivate them toward the *independent* pursuit of knowledge.

Examining 12,132 audiovisual items for damage and returning them to their proper place after use.

Preparing materials for teachers in the audio-visual areas (tapes and transparencies) where these materials are not available.

Checking out books to primary students.

Helping all students find materials on their reading and interest levels.

Dusting and cleaning libraries.	Meeting faculty requests for materials, student bibliographers, skills and unit classes.
Counting cards for circulation reports.	Helping students to acquire the skills vital for independent study activities.
Turning down teacher requests for materials that are not available.	Selecting and ordering materials in deficient areas.

Recommendations

To achieve the kind of materials center program that is vitally needed, we must have:

1. Space in each materials center to accommodate a minimum of 100 students.
2. A full-time librarian and full-time library aide in each school.

Daily memos similar to the foregoing, plus countless meetings, plus the most effective use possible of the time each librarian has in a school, will usually bring results. These results may not include full staffing overnight, but each professional staff member gained is a battle won. Trained staff members do not replace the volunteers but do direct the activities of the volunteers toward the necessary clerical and housekeeping tasks, thus releasing the professional's time for work with students and teachers.

Hiring Procedures: The Job Seeker's Waltz

Patrons of most large school districts should be comforted by the fact that the greatest care is usually taken in the hiring of personnel. The applicant for a particular job (who goes through a minimum of four to eight traumatic interviews) is not as comforted by this fact. The job seeker's waltz goes something as illustrated here:

Step One	*Step Two*	*Step Three*
Director of Personnel	to Library Supervisor	to Director of Elementary Education
	Step Four to One or two or more Principals	
Step Five Back to Director of Personnel	*Step Six* Back to Director of Elementary Curriculum	*Step Seven* To the Asst. Superintendent
	Step Eight Supt. of Schools (and contract)	

Of course, at each step, the applicant's personnel folder is forwarded to the interviewer who, during the interview, scowls occasionally at the material contained therein. Each interviewer also adds to the folder his comments concerning the applicant, and the job seeker's waltz can come to a halt at any step along the way should two or more interviewers be displeased with the applicant. In talking with applicants for the job of elementary school librarian, each interviewer has his own set of prejudices concerning the role the librarian is to play in the school. These prejudices are determined through concepts developed from past experiences (or lack of same) with the elementary materials center program and by the goals of a particular district's program. While there are some exceptions, applicants usually are of four types:

Type One: The "I've Had It" Applicant

This job seeker is usually a classroom teacher who is sure that an elementary librarian has little to do, and therefore the library job would be a "rest" from the classroom. It has

Eureka! A Staff of Twelve

never dawned on her that a good elementary librarian is a MASTER TEACHER whose classroom is the school of 700+ children.

Type Two: The "I've Had It" Applicant

This is a variation of the "type one" applicant except that instead of being a classroom teacher, she is a secondary librarian looking for a place to spend her retirement years.

Type Three: The Sweet Young Thing

This little girl is right out of the library school and while she may someday be an excellent librarian, she must first gain experience in the classroom if she is to be truly effective "teacher of teachers."

Type Four: The Ideal Applicant

The ideal applicant is that rare experienced teacher or professional librarian who clearly sees the tremendous potential of the IMC program and whose eyes light up with energy and enthusiasm as the potential is discussed.

If the library supervisor has this same energy and enthusiasm for her job (and she wouldn't last long in the job if she didn't) she can usually spot it in others.

A Word of Explanation

Over the past few years considerable debate has echoed in the halls of state and national librarian's organizations concerning the professional status of school librarians. While the ideal school librarian would have his or her undergraduate degree in Education and the Masters Degree in Library Science, this is not generally the case. Whether a teacher who has gone back to school for training in the library field (but who does not have the fifth year degree) is a "professional" librarian or not, is not as important to those in the schools who do the hiring as it seems to be to the ALA. What is important is a YES answer to the following four questions:

1. Does she have a good, working knowledge of the school library field to do the job?

2. Has she had successful experience in the classroom to enable her to understand and work effectively with students and teachers?

3. Is she a dedicated and enthusiastic individual who fully believes that the work she will be doing is of vital importance?

4. Does she have a genuine liking for people and an inherent respect for the dignity of each individual?

If the following quiz could be given to every applicant, the answers to these questions would be quickly apparent.

The Learning Resource Center's Director

Directions: Place a check before what you consider to be the *four* most important aspects of the Director's job.

_____ 1. Catalog and classify all print and nonprint materials to assure easy accessibility by students and teachers.

_____ 2. Train and supervise both adult and student media center aides in efficient library/media center routines.

_____ 3. Establish and maintain efficient circulation procedures for all materials.

_____ 4. Develop reserve collections of print and nonprint materials on teacher request.

_____ 5. Select and acquire hardware and software for the learning center and establish hardware specifications for the school.

_____ 6. Maintain hardware in usable condition and establish a workable schedule of repair, and replacement.

_____ 7. Produce, or assist teachers in the production of instructional materials (tapes, transparencies, etc.) to meet specific needs.

_____ 8. Train and schedule student aides in the operation of hardware to assist teachers and train teachers, where possible, in efficient operation and utilization of hardware.

_____ 9. Be able to define the educational needs of the school as they relate to the curriculum, organizational structures for learning, faculty requests and student interests.

_____10. Introduce to classes materials to be utilized in units of work and introduce the skills necessary for efficient use of these materials.

_____11. Provide direct assistance to individuals or groups of students in the research process regardless of the carrier of knowledge used.

_____12. Work cooperatively with the classroom teacher in developing meaningful and relevant IMC activities for her students based on specific behavioral objectives.

Explanation of the Quiz

Library/media personnel generally see themselves in one of three postures. Items one through four describe the traditional, stereotyped school librarian whose concern is more with order than with use of materials. While the point is well taken that good organization is essential for easy accessibility of materials by students and teachers, organization is only the *means* by which the good school librarian can do her job. It is not the sum and total of the job.

Items five through eight describe another kind of stereotype. This is the audiovisual director who tinkers with machines all day, having little knowledge (and caring less) about the ultimate educational use of the hardware under his care.

Items nine through twelve describe the professional library/media person who is needed in the schools today. This "Media Specialist" sees equipment and materials (and the organization of same) as vehicles for learning, and places the learning process above all other priorities in the library/media center. In hiring this breed of educator for the school materials center, few administrators realize that they have acquired in their schools a catalyst for change. The experienced library supervisor who has recommended the hiring of this librarian realizes full well that her forces have been strengthened in the battle for improvement.

Portrait of An Elementary Librarian

In addition to being knowledgeable and enthusiastic, the elementary librarian must possess other qualities for success in the job:

1. She must have tact and the ability to suggest new ideas and materials to classroom teachers without the slightest hint that she might be telling the teacher how to teach.

2. She must have extraordinary powers of deductive reasoning, as, for example, knowing that when a five-year old asks for a book on "engines" he does not mean the type found in a car. He does mean "Indians."

3. A terrific memory helps as she is bombarded with eighteen

requests from teachers as she makes her way down the hall between the rest room and the library.

4. She should be an actress at storytelling time, a mother when children become frustrated, and a boxing coach to break up occasional fights.

5. She should be a gadgeteer when machines won't behave, a bookkeeper in figuring out and keeping track of school budget procedures, and

6. She should be able to afford a sturdy pair of sneakers (or roller skates) since she will move at a dead run all day.

Scheduling the Staff: "Musical Schools"

Hopefully, a growing district library/media program means additions to the staff each year until such time as a desired level of service is reached. Staff needs should not be estimated toward an ultimate set number of personnel, but rather should be projected on a two- to three-year basis. Both State and National Standards should be considered as goals, but not as ultimate goals. As the staff grows and as teachers become involved in the IMC program, students will also become fully involved. When the point is reached that the materials center has become truly the hub of the educational process, demands for service will continue to grow, for the possibilities for service in such a center are limitless.

The major problem which exists in increasing staff each year (until the point is reached when each school has at least one professional library/media person on its staff) is the lack of identity between the librarian and the teachers and pupils she is to serve. The necessary task of becoming well versed with the contents of a particular materials collection takes longer than one year, especially if the librarian is serving more than one school. Becoming well acquainted with faculty and students is another important factor in good library service which cannot be accomplished overnight. When the staff is increased, it follows that librarians who have been serving three or four schools will only be serving one or two schools. While this lessened workload is good, it does mean a readjustment of personnel through-

Eureka! A Staff of Twelve

out the schools and the task of beginning again to build good working relationships with teachers and pupils.

Another problem which arises with less than full staffing in a school (as can be noted from an examination of the schedule on the next page) is the necessity that arises at times for two librarians to serve a single school. For example: School No. 7 is entitled to 7 half-days of service (based on student enrollment). The district policy on scheduling, however, states that no school shall have less than half-time service since ten librarians are available to serve fourteen buildings. This means that the librarian in school No. 7 will serve seven half days in that school and three half days in another school. Since this second school is entitled to five half days of service, a second librarian will serve the additional two half days. If this seems somewhat confusing, working out a fair and equitable schedule which will keep everyone as happy as possible is one more of the many tasks of the supervisor.

Each librarian who spends most of her time in one school and simply fills in the gaps in another, tends to feel that she really only has one school and, consequently, does not make the effort in the smaller school to give the quality of service expected in the larger school. Teachers and pupils, seeing two librarians moving in and out of the building are not sure with whom to identify, and keeping track of confusing schedules simply adds one more burden to the teacher's already busy day. Thus, the library is not used as effectively as it could be.

The Supervisor's Role in Relation to the Professional Staff

Most administrative personnel are accused at one time or another of spending their time chatting, smoking cigars, going to lunch, or occasionally taking a moment from their life of leisure to fill out a report or two. Because they are somewhat removed from the academic scene, it is simply assumed by many that they don't do very much. It never seems to occur to some faculty members that buildings do not spring forth from the ground by osmosis, nor do operating funds (and paychecks) come from some hidden pot of gold. Constructing buildings, securing operating funds, budgeting, planning educational goals, and implementing these goals through a careful blending of staff, facilities, and materials requires the time and effort of a number of individuals whose decisions *do* have a far reaching impact on the education of the district's students.

As a member of the administrative team, the Elementary Supervisor generally works directly under the Superintendent in Charge of Instruction. While the responsibility for the total elementary learning resources program of the district is centered in her office, she may or may not have responsibility for the evaluation of library/media center staff members throughout the schools. Many supervisors feel that while they do have a responsibility for developing guidelines and criteria for the evaluation of library/media staff members, that the actual evaluation should be done by other administrative personnel of the district. The reasons for this are twofold:

1. The principal of each building will become more aware of the type of library/media service offered in his building if evaluation of staff members is his responsibility, and

2. The library supervisor can establish a closer working relationship with other members of the library/media staff if she does not carry the responsibility for evaluation of their job performance.

The role of the supervisor in relation to the staff is to set the pace or provide the leadership for programs to be carried out cooperatively throughout the district. She suggests rather than demands improvements to be made in the program, and serves as both resource person and trouble shooter for the individual programs throughout the district. Legitimate calls for help and service will not be forthcoming if the librarian feels that in asking for help, she is indicating that she is less than totally effective in her position. The supervisor who does not evaluate the work of staff members is in a far better position to be accepted as a member of a team working together to improve the district's library services.

Eureka! A Staff of Twelve 57

BLANK SCHOOL DISTRICT

SCHEDULE FOR RESOURCE CENTER PERSONNEL   DATE _____

MEDIA SPECIALIST		MONDAY Office	TUESDAY Office	WEDNESDAY	THURSDAY Office	FRIDAY Office
A	AM	1	Office	1	1	1
	PM		Office			3
B	AM	3	2	2	2	2
	PM	2	3	3	3	4
C	AM	4	1	1	4	4
	PM	4	4	4	4	5
D	AM	5	5	5	5	5
	PM	5	5	5	5	6
E	AM	6	6	6	6	6
	PM	6	6	6	6	8
F	AM	8	7	8	7	7
	PM	7	7	7	7	9
G	AM	9	9	9	9	9
	PM	9	9	3	9	11
H	AM	11	11	10	11	11
	PM	10	11	11	11	12
I	AM	12	12	12	12	12
	PM	12	8	12	8	10
J	AM	13	10	13	13	13
	PM	13	13	13	10	

Monthly Staff Meetings

If the elementary materials centers program is to achieve a measure of uniformity, there must be communication among the staff members located in each school. Communication in the form of a monthly staff meeting is valuable for a number of reasons.

1. Ideas and problems can be shared and discussed. In this way, each staff member will not have the feeling that she alone is inventing the wheel.
2. Responsibility for covering review sources for both print and non-print materials can be shared, avoiding duplication of effort.
3. New materials received in one school (but perhaps not in another) can be evaluated and discussed (and, if desirable, examined).
4. Changes in uniform procedures can be discussed and debated and a consensus of opinion reached, rather than coming as a direct (and perhaps undesirable) order from the supervisor.
5. Time can be allocated for visits by salesmen or for displays of materials for examination relieving the librarians from the necessity of snatching a minute from their busy school schedules to talk with salesmen or preview new materials.
6. Minor bookkeeping details, problems with orders and any upcoming activities can be discussed and ironed out.

The Monthly Report

There is considerable debate among library supervisors as to the value of the monthly report required of the librarian in each school. Some supervisors feel that statistics are not necessary and that the school librarian's time can better be spent in duties related directly to good library/media center service.

Other supervisors feel that their fight for additional staff, or space, or materials, or whatever the current need may be, is strengthened by the existence of such statistics. In addition, these supervisors feel that such reports can indicate signs of a successful program, or conversely, point out trouble areas which may need assistance. Statistical reports need not be a chore for the school librarian if she will set aside a few minutes at the end of each day to complete each day's statistics. This few minutes of thought concerning the activities of her day may prove most beneficial. In noting the number of teacher requests received, she may also note those teachers who are not making requests. Should the circulation of audiovisual materials begin to show an increase, it may indicate a need for more materials of this type. If no one is requesting that she introduce materials for students beginning a new unit of work, she may want to begin an investigation to find out why. If a very successful activity occurred that day, she may want to make a note to try the activity with other students or teachers. The monthly report then can serve as a daily self-evaluation of one's work.

The Library Service Center

As the professional staff of the district's elementary libraries begins to grow, the supervisor will find that there is less demand from the schools for direct services, but more demand for supportive services. Few elementary libraries have sufficient professional and clerical staff. Yet, a good elementary library program demands the same level of service, if not a higher level of service, as the best secondary program. The supportive services of the supervisor can directly affect the level of service in each school by relieving the professional staff of many of the necessary administrative and organizational duties in order that they may devote time to working with children and teachers.

Through the establishment of a district-wide elementary processing and service center (or better yet, if agreement with the secondary staff can be reached, district-wide processing and services for all schools) much of the workload of the staff in the schools can be relieved. It is possible for a service center for ten to fifteen elementary schools to operate in a space equal to one classroom. If, in the processing of materials, printed cards are ordered and used, from eighteen to twenty thousand items per year can be processed by a staff of two plus providing the other supportive services which are outlined in the sample service center annual report which follows:

Report on the Activities of
The Elementary Library Service Center and
The Elementary Library Supervisor

_____

Date

1. *Curriculum Activities*
   In serving as the supportive "right arm" of the elementary librarians, the staff of the processing center composes, produces and duplicates nearly all materials used by students, teachers and librarians which are a part of the library program in the elementary schools. Among these materials are:

   a) Manual for teaching library skills; K-2
   b) Manual for teaching library skills: 3-6
   c) Bibliographies to accompany each Reading unit for pupils 3-6 (36 units)
   d) Unite bibliographies for use by students
   e) Kindergarten Program for developing library readiness (for use by teachers)
   f) Tape/Transparency series for teaching library skills (10 series)
   g) All forms needed for efficient library organization and management used by the elementary librarians (inrequest forms, overdue notices, book report forms, forms for independent study activities, etc.)
   h) Literature & Skill Sheets
   i) Tape Recordings

2. *Processing Activities*
   The library center handles ordering, receipt and processing of nearly all of the materials placed in the elementary centers and for the private schools in the district under Title II. This provides for uniformity of processing, relieves the elementary librarians of clerical and cataloging tasks in order that they may spend their time with students, and provides a considerable saving in processing costs to the district.

3. *Professional Library*
   The staff of the processing center handles the cataloging, processing and circulation of the district's professional library located in the processing center. Every other year a complete printed book catalog

Eureka! A Staff of Twelve

of the holdings of the professional library is complied and distributed to every teacher in the district. Requests are handled in person, by phone or by interschool mail.

4. *Federal Programs*
   Materials for all public and private schools are ordered, received and processed in the center. All records and a complete shelf list of holdings are kept up-to-date in the center. The coordinator makes numerous trips a year to the private schools to confer with private school principals on their orders.

5. *Staff of the Center*
   The center staff consists of one full-time secretary, the elementary library supervisor, and additional staff as needed.
   The center operates the year around.

6. *Elementary Library Supervisor*
   The elementary supervisor accepts full responsibility for the activities of the processing center. She handles all cataloging of materials for which printed cards are not available. She supervises the processing of materials and prepares all unit worksheets, bibliographies, forms, and all other printed material required by the elementary librarians in their work. She issues selection lists of new materials, conducts volunteer workshops, interprets the IMC program to visitors, works on curriculum committees considering new materials, plans workshops for teachers and librarians, assists in planning new library quarters and developing new programs, provides any needed assistance to the elementary librarians on request, prepares federal and state reports, maintains all records and works with public and private school personnel concerned with federal library programs.

7. *Visitors and Workshops*
   Media personnel and administrators from the following school districts have visited the district and observed the Program in action:

   > List all institutions, agencies,
   > and individuals here.

   Workshops presenting the district's Program were done by the Supervisor and Staff at the request of the following schools or agencies:

   > List all workshops, talks, public
   > appearances, etc., here

Staffing the Service Center

One of the most important staff positions in the elementary library/media program is that of the service center secretary. In addition to being a jack-of-all-trades, she must must be able to work with the supervisor, the professional staff, and the administrators of all of the elementary schools. Her job is one of the most demanding in the district, yet she must be able to "keep her cool" on those days when she is swamped and additional requests for service are received. Just as it was cited earlier, since many administrators feel that "anyone" can be an elementary librarian, the feeling also prevails that "anyone" can work in the processing/service center. While it is doubtful that administrators have given any thought to the matter, it should be obvious that bibliographies, unit sheets, correspondence, materials orders, tapes, transparencies, and skills materials do not emerge from the clouds. Nor do books and other instructional materials make their way from the printing press to the library shelves, ready for circulation, all by themselves. How delightful it would be if this were so! Thus a key person in the service center is the secretary/technician who both supervises and performs technical processing operations.

It is most important to furnish the director of personnel with a written description of the qualifications and duties of the service center secretary unless one wants to be placed in the position of one supervisor whose superior hired a "housewife type" friend for the job. After one week of training in the processing of materials, this lady (before quitting) caught the ear of her good friend, the superintendent, and proceeded to carry on about the inefficient way materials were prepared for district libraries. To her mind, "all those silly numbers and cards" weren't necessary at all. The supervisor was a bit startled the following morning when the superintendent paid a visit to the service center to inquire about its "inefficient" operation. The service center secretary description is provided here in order that other supervisors might avoid a similar traumatic experience.

Job Description: The Library Service Center Secretary

1. Education: High School Graduate with Additional Secretarial Training.

2. Experience: One (1) year in library technical processing services or two years of college training in the library/media field.

3. Personal Characteristics Desired: Minimum age 21. Good health, neat in appearance, clear use of language, poise in dealing with teachers, administrators, media personnel, educators from other school districts as well as within the district, and with the general public.

4. Duties and Skills

Secretarial Duties
Handles correspondence
Prepares schedules and forms
Orders and inventories instructional supplies
Handles requests of media personnel and educators from other districts
Keeps appointment schedule of supervisor

Clerical Duties
Typing and filing of correspondence
  bibliographies
  reports
  unit materials
  orders
  workshop materials
  skills booklets
  curriculum guides
  notices
  memos
  requisitions
  bulletins

Technical Processing
Checks orders received against invoices
Handles final disposition of purchase orders and invoices
Checks for availability of processing kits and matches with materials
When kits are not available, types catalog cards, charge cards and pockets
Glues pockets
Applies call number to spine
Accessions materials
Separates and alphabetizes catalog cards to be sent to schools with materials
Stamps ownership marks on all materials

Professional Library
Handles all educator requests for materials from professional library.
Issues professional library bibliographies
Charges, discharges and renews materials
Processes new additions
Informs patrons of overdue materials

Miscellaneous Duties
Verifies ordering data
Runs machine tapes on orders
Assigns copy numbers
Processes records for materials withdrawn from title II collection
Maintains equipment inventories
Routes processed materials to schools
Inspects materials for damage

"Goofs" Supervisors Make

In dealing with a professional and clerical staff, school administrators, teachers and parents, it is the rare supervisor who has not "goofed" at one time or another. Among the most common types of goofs are the following:

GOOF	EXAMPLE
1. Assume because you think you know what you are doing, that everyone else does, too.	You may know why School A has its materials processed before School B. But does the administrator of School B know why (and agree with your reasoning)?
2. Assume that because a written memo has been issued to the staff concerning an activity, that follow-through will be automatic.	A memo is issued to the principals at the beginning of the school year listing librarian's monthly meeting dates and times. Unless a reminder is sent each month the day before the meeting, someone will be looking for his librarian.

Eureka! A Staff of Twelve

3. Assume that because you are enthusiastic about a project or idea that all of the library staff will be also.	Imagine the surprise of a supervisor who arranged for in-service training of teachers by the library staff, to find that staff members were less than anxious to become public speakers . . . even on the subject of libraries.
4. Assume that because uniform programs, processing and materials have been developed for the schools in the district that the district program is uniform.	Each school's program is under the direction of a librarian who is a unique individual with her own way of doing things. What is important to the supervisor may not be important to the librarian and vise versa.

However, when the point is reached in a school district when every elementary school has a trained librarian and sufficient clerical staff, the occasional headaches of staff supervision are overshadowed by the reality of an effective program.

Titles Mentioned in this Chapter

Lindgren, Astrid. *Pippi Longstocking.* Viking 1950

School Media Standards. Missouri State Department of Education. Jefferson City, Mo. June 1969

Arron, Shirley Louise. "A Review of Selected Research Studies in School Librarianship 1967-1971." *School Libraries.* Summer 1972

Sullivan, Peggy, Ed. *Realization: The Final Report of the Knapp School Libraries Project.* American Library Association. 1969

4

UNCLE SAM HATES LIBRARY SUPERVISORS:
BIDS, BUDGETS AND BUREAUCRACY

Alice in Purchase Order Land
While the requirements for certification as a school librarian or library supervisor differ considerably among the states, most requirements include courses in administration, book selection, children's or adolescent literature, reference, cataloging, and, perhaps, an audiovisual course. An additional, and most essential course which should be required, is instruction in accounting and in the administration and operation of the school district purchasing department. (For more specific requirements, see *A Manual on Certification Requirements for School Personnel in the USA*. NEA 1971)

Since most school districts come under the classification of big business based on the amount of money spent in a district in a given year, the expenditure and accounting of funds becomes a major operation. Most supervisors, having entered the administrative position via the classroom or library situation are ill prepared for this world of higher finance.

One of the most valuable allies the supervisor can have in a district is the Director of Purchasing, who generally has the power of the purse. Working under him is a secretary, who handles communications on bids and expenditures, a purchasing agent who (hopefully) keeps track of purchase orders and invoices, a head bookkeeper, who keeps accounts and pays bills, and numerous supportive clerical staff. To follow a purchase order through this financial maze is, indeed, enlightening.

Uncle Sam Hates Library Supervisors

1. The librarian in the school writes a purchase order. The order indicates the item and cost, where the item is to be delivered and the account to which it is to be charged.

2. The purchase order is sent to the principal who approves and initials it.

3. The purchase order moves to the library supervisor who approves and initials it.

4. It then goes to the director of purchasing who approves and initials it.

5. The purchasing agent receives the order, records it, and sends one copy to the dealer, keeps one copy, and sends copies to the bookkeeper, the library supervisor and the librarian who originated the order.

6. When the item and invoice for payment are received, they are marked "ok" and initialed by the librarian and sent to the purchasing agent.

7. The purchasing agent "oks" payment for the bookkeeper who enters the payment in the district's books and makes out the check, which is forwarded to the vendor.

While this procedure may appear fairly simple, those who deal with it daily know that all types of dire happenings can occur between steps one and seven. Among the most common occurances are the following:

1. The principal makes out a purchase order (charged to the library account) without the librarian's knowledge, and the librarian, who is hopefully keeping careful records of her expenditures, thinks she has funds to spend which are already spent.

2. The secretary typing the order makes a typographical error in placing the correct account code on the order and an order for School A is paid out of School B's account. This, bringing about all sorts of jolly repercussions from the principal of School B.

3. The order is rejected by the library supervisor and returned to the school by the library supervisor for one of the following reasons:

a. The order is not balanced in accordance with the needs of the collection.
b. Quality of materials ordered is questionable.
c. Order exceeds the school allocation.
d. Other. (This covers a host of uncataloged sins)

4. An incomplete order is received by the librarian who assumes all shorts have been cancelled. It is paid and closed in the accounts and the leftover funds are expended for another item. Three months later the missing items (and bill for same) arrive.

5. A 1970 dealer's catalog was used for a 1974 order. Price increases, while not shown in the old catalog, appear on the invoice, the bill being a considerably larger amount than the amount encumbered to pay the bill.

6. The items listed for payment on the dealer's invoice and the items actually received bear no resemblance to each other.

Each snafu must, of course, be dealt with by the library supervisor in one way or another. One example will suffice to demonstrate the role of the supervisor as a trouble shooter in this area.

Librarian A orders a group of math models for a hundred dollars. Three months later the items have not arrived and Librarian A discovers that her account is in the red. She writes a letter to the company asking them to cancel the order. A copy of the letter goes to the supervisor. The company replies by stating that the items in question were sent to the school district two weeks after the order was received and a copy of the bill is enclosed. The bill, incidentally, is for $150. Librarian A panics, having visions of this amount being taken from her next pay check.

Enters the supervisor. She (1) checks with the delivery agent who okayed receipt of the order. He does not remember where in the district the order was routed; (2) checks with all math departments in the district's schools to ascertain if any department has acquired any new mathematics models lately; (3) Discovers that the Secondary School Math Coordinator has been wondering for two months where these nice new models had come from . . .

and in the two month period had distributed them throughout the secondary buildings; (4) Takes a sneaky look at the amount of money available in the math department's account and discovers they are loaded! (5) Explains the problem to the director of purchasing, who, after a chat with the math coordinator, transfers the encumbrance to that department's account (from which it is paid.)

Had the problem not had such a happy ending, if, for example, the material had not been located or the funds not have been available, the supervisor would then have written the company guaranteeing payment of the bill on July 1 (the beginning of the fiscal year). Funds from the coming year's budget would have been used to pay the bill whether materials were located or not since the company did have proof of delivery.

Life With the Computer

The world of the computer has been with us for some time. School districts who have moved to computerized ordering, processing, and inventory procedures are generally enthusiastic about the capabilities of the computer in lessening the workload of the library staff, cutting administrative costs, and decreasing the time between the ordering of materials and the circulation of these same materials. It is a marvelous age of computerized information retrieval where programmers, through describing a specific set of functions to a second generation computer, have enabled it to design the third generation computer. One function, however, at least from the library supervisor's point of view, that these mechanical monsters have not yet been programmed to perform is that of straightening out a "fouled up" materials order. As one salesman put it, "I keep telling that computer that we have problems with your order, but all it says is 'click, click, click.'"

The "Picture Book Caper" will suffice to illustrate the problems the supervisor has in this area of computerized ordering. Data are provided chronologically to lessen the confusion of the reader.

December 1972
8 sets (on four different purchase orders) of picture books were ordered from a well-known company.

May 1973
7 sets had arrived. Six sets were paid for. Payment on the final purchase order was held up and the following letter sent:

Dear Sir:
   We received only one (1) set of Picture Books on our purchase order s 80-870. We have been billed for two sets. Please send the second set of books in order that we can pay your invoice in full.

Sincerely,

July 1973
Since all other purchase orders had been paid, the total amount owed the company was $20.00. (The second set of books having not yet arrived). Payment was sent to the company for the $20.00 owed for one set of books received.

January 1974
A computer print-out bill was received in the amount of $40.00. A letter was sent informing the company that all amounts owed to the company had been paid.

March 1974
Computer print-out bill for $40.00 received. Letter sent as follows:

Dear Sir:
   Enclosed is your invoice dated March 1974. It does not list a purchase order number. Also enclosed are copies of my last letter to you. We have not received an answer to the letter and cannot pay invoices unless you identify them by using our purchase order numbers.

Sincerely,

June 1974
Computer print-out bill received for $40.00. Copy of the March 1974 letter sent in reply with note below added:

Dear Sir:
   Our records show we do not owe you any money. Please check prior correspondence.

Sincerely,

Uncle Sam Hates Library Supervisors

July 1974
Bill received in the amount of $80.00. Ignored.

November 1974
Bill received in the amount of $20.00. Ignored.

January 1975
The following computer print-out letter received from the company:

Dear Board of Education:
   You have ignored our previous letter requesting payment of $80.00 on your delinquent account. Avoid further collection activity by sending your payment immediately.

Late January 1975
   Letter received:
Dear Customer:
   Our records have been corrected and now show full credit for payments you sent us.

                                                Sincerely

March 1975
Letter Received (Computer print-out)
Dear Board of Education:
   The records of our computer center show a balance due on your account in the amount of $80.00. The amount due is required to be paid by March 30, 1975.

April 1975
Letter Received: Computer print out
Dear Board of Education:
   Payment has not been received on your delinquent account. This is your final notice before we forward your account to our local collection agency.

                                                Sincerely,
May 1975
   Telephone call received from the local collection agency. The supervisor carefully explained the whole computerized series of events. Copies of all correspondence were forwarded to the agency with copies of all purchase orders and cancelled checks showing full payment, along with the fervent hope that personnel of the collection agency would be able to locate a human being in the

computerized world of the large company in question. Comment from the agency: "You know, we have trouble getting those people to talk to us, too!"

The Grey-Haired Femme Fatale

No discussion on budgeting, purchase orders and bids would be complete without a word concerning salesmen. The migratory habits of book salesmen coincide with those times of the year when funds are received by the librarian for purchase of materials. While many school libraries place orders the year around, the bulk of the ordering is generally done in the spring with additional ordering done when federal funds are received in the late fall or winter. While many salesmen represent reputable, professional companies and take a professional approach to showing their wares, the field does abound with that second breed of salesman representing a "fly by night" company, or no company at all. This second type can generally be identified by his "Hi, doll, how's tricks" approach. Should the truth be known, middle-aged, grey-haired supervisors who have been in their jobs for any length of time, have been offered everything from a drink to an apartment down the street, and the bigger the budget the supervisor has with which to work, the more frequent (and interesting) the offers!

The three most common pitches of the "fly by night" salesman are:

The preferred customer pitch. Since your district is a "preferred customer" you will receive a 50% discount on all books ordered. All you have to do is order in sets. The supervisor who bites on this offer will find that the "sets of quality library books" contain paperbacks, trade bindings, ancient copyrights, and publishers cast-offs.

The "Immediate, if not sooner delivery" approach. This salesman "guarantees" a hundred percent delivery of any books ordered to be delivered within two weeks. To substantiate his claim he places a person-to-person "long distance" call to the president of the company to give the supervisor direct assurance of his claim "from the top." The supervisor who falls for this gambit will probably find herself talking to a friend of the salesman located in a phone booth down the street. The hundred percent delivery frequently changes to fifty percent or less due to "circumstances beyond the company's control." The "two weeks" delivery promise often grows to six months or more.

The *"Send in for approval"* or *"Leave for examination"* approach. This salesman has read library school textbooks. He stresses the need for personal examination of materials before purchase and either leaves the materials or has them sent "on approval." This is, of course, standard practice with reputable companies. However, while the reputable company will accept return of the materials or arrange for their salesman to pick them up, the "fly by night" company will simply bill the district for the materials and refuse return of them.

It is essential, then, for the supervisor to know the companies and their representatives with whom she deals and to avoid the temptation to accept "pie-in-the-sky" offers. Close communication with other supervisors in the area can be helpful in developing a list of reputable companies and salesmen.

This same close communication has often resulted in supervisors from districts meeting together on a regular basis to exchange information and ideas. For example, in St. Louis County, Missouri, the library supervisors' group maintains close contact with the Suburban Media Directors' Association and annually these two groups sponsor a library/media exhibit to which reputable salesmen are invited. Each salesman attending is given the opportunity to display his wares throughout the day at the exhibit attended by administrators, teachers and library media personnel from all twenty-nine school districts in the County. Further contacts are made by individual districts with the companies represented by the salesmen when the district has an interest in purchasing a particular item.

Bid, Bid, Who's Got the Bid?

While books, software, and smaller items are generally ordered through the purchase order route described previously, furniture equipment and larger items are purchased through a system of bids. Simply put, the school district makes its needs known to a number of companies who might be able to fill these needs, and the company quoting the best price generally gets the order. However, before the district reaches the point of letting bids, these needs must be determined. Most districts do this through the combined efforts of principal/administrator committees called "priority committees." The work of the priority committee consists of taking a look at one certain area (the library/media center, for example) and determining the furniture and equipment considered basic to its operation. This is one district committee on which the library supervisor's presence is essential. If an item does not appear on the district's priority list, it cannot be ordered. Thus, the supervisor will want to make sure that at least the following items are included as standard furniture and equipment for an elementary library/media center.

Furniture and Equipment Priority List
Elementary Materials Centers

charge counter
step stool
magazine rack
dictionary stand
card catalog
book truck
charging trays
tables
chairs
legal size file cabinet
filmstrip cabinet
card sorter
pencil sharpener
waste can
shelving
record storage cabinet
cassette tape storage
   cabinet
study print storage cabinet
book ends

typewriter
super 8mm projector
Television with stand
opaque projector
35mm slide projector
   80 tray
micro-projector
filmstrip projector
overhead projector
record player
listening stations hot press
filmstrip viewers
cassette recorder
reel to reel recorder
microfilm readers tacking
   iron
sound filmstrip viewers
projection screen
16mm projector
projection stand

Eureka! A Staff of Twelve

Once the items have made their way to the priority list, each school is surveyed by the supervisor to determine the amount of each item needed. A list of furniture and equipment needed in each school is submitted to the Director of Purchasing and specifications and cost estimates are developed for each item. If funds are not available to meet all needs, the supervisor must determine the most essential needs. This is referred to as "the supervisor on a tightrope" phase of the operation since each school feels that its needs ARE the most essential. Once determined, however, the bid is ready to be let.

Preparing the Bid Offer

Steps in preparing the offer to companies to bid on various amounts of specific items differ among school districts. However, a fairly standard procedure is as follows:

1. A list of items is developed giving exact specifications of items desired. It is not sufficient to merely specify that bids are wanted on 80 sections of library shelving. The height, width, depth, type of wood and other pertinent information must be included. Exact specifications should be similar to those listed below:

> Double-faced Shelving, Natural Wood, aisle type, 42" H x 36" L x 24" D, 2 adjustable shelves, 1 fixed base shelf each side.   Bro-Dart #60-991-1 or equal.
>
> Single Faced Shelving Initial Units, Natural 72" H x 36" L x 12" D.   Educator #627-36.
>
> Record Storage Cabinets, tan metal floor units, 30" W x 14" D x 48" H.   Smith system #53 or equal.
>
> Card catalogs, 12-drawer wooden, natural color, Bro-Dart #60-880 or equal.
>
> Filmstrip Cabinet, brown metal with extension arms, 10 " L x 10 " W x 17 " D.   Coffey #200 or equal.
>
> 4-Drawer legal size file cabinets, desert sand color, 17⅞" W x 26⅝" D x 52¼" H.   Bro-Dart Regular, or equal.

2. Once specifications are developed for each item desired, the total number of items needed by the District in each category is determined.
3. Information sent to the vendor should be as follows:
   a. The name and address of the person to whom the bid is to be submitted.
   b. Final date for submission of bids.
   c. The amount of the Cashier's check to accompany the quotation. (Such checks are returned to unsuccessful bidders.)
   d. How the bid is to be submitted.
   e. Conditions to be met if installation or assembly of furniture or equipment is necessary. (Liability Insurance is usually one of these conditions.)
   f. Statement concerning the submission of samples for consideration by district personnel.
   g. Terms and place of delivery.
   h. Instructions to bid separately on each item rather than submitting an overall bid for all items.
   i. Instructions concerning substitution of items where a specific item or manufacturer is requested.
   j. A statement affirming the right of the School District to reject any or all bids and to be the sole authority on determining the best bid.

Careful records should be maintained in the office of the supervisor concerning the furniture and equipment needs of each library/media center. Records should be updated as items are received or transferred from one building to another in order that basic needs can be met as rapidly as possible. In addition, all concerned library/media personnel should be consulted on specifications when new type of furniture or equipment is contemplated for addition to the centers. If possible, samples should be placed on display and time arranged for personnel to view and submit written comments on their preferences. If a great difference of opinion exists among the staff in deciding on a particular item, a meeting should be held where the merits and drawbacks of each item are discussed and a consensus reached. Staff members must achieve an understanding that only through uniformity of equipment and furniture purchases can savings in the purchase of these items be realized.

Planning Ahead

School districts operating on a fiscal year determine the furniture and equipment needs for a building approximately one year before the furniture and equipment are delivered to the building. Needs are determined in October or November of one school year, bids are let in May or June of the same school year, and equipment which is supposed to be delivered before the opening of school in the fall is likely to arrive at almost anytime during that following school year. It is approximately one to one and a half years from the time the need is determined until the need is met. This is one excellent reason for a *personal* survey of each library/media center's needs by the library supervisor. Without such long-range planning, the school librarian may find the library/media center with filmstrips and no projectors, books and no shelves, microfilm and no readers, etc. Planning must take into account not only present programs and facilities but future programs and expanded facilities.

Budgeting for Materials

Planned uniform growth of materials collections is essential if increased demands for service by pupils and teachers are to be met. Specific items to be ordered are determined by the librarian in each school in working with the faculty and students of the school. The overall budget amount for the school must be determined by the librarian and library supervisor of the district, and submitted and justified to the administration by the supervisor.

Budget estimates are made based on what are considered to be desirable goals for library/media collections. The goals set by the 1969 *Standards for School Media Programs* (a joint effort of the American Association of School Librarians and the AECT) and the 1975 *Media Programs: District and School* which places stress on the functions of the media center, are highly desirable. A survey of the rationale behind the Standards can be found in the Spring 1973 *School Media Quarterly*.) Many states within the past few years have developed their own standards for required media collections and some states will rate the quality of the district's educational program (in part) by the effort that has been made to achieve the state's standards.

Both the librarian in the school and the library supervisor should know the state and national standards. If a school district does not meet the state standards, these must be the basis for determining the quantitative amount of materials needed for a particular center. To develop a long range plan for budgeting, the information needed by the library supervisor from each school librarian in the district would include the following:

1. The present status of the materials collection. Included would be the number of books, filmstrips, films, recordings, periodical subscriptions, and other instructional media.
2. The number of items required by state standards in each category.
3. The estimated unit cost per item.
4. The estimated number of items to be received from all sources of funds for the remainder of the school year
5. The actual number of items needed to reach state standards.

When these figures are received, the supervisor double checks the state requirements and compares the requirements with the materials on hand and estimated number of materials to be received. A uniform per item cost should be determined by the supervisor before information is compiled in the schools in order that every librarian works with the same cost estimates. The total cost for each school to reach standards is then calculated.

In addition to determining budget needs to meet specific standards, there are other considerations. Collections must be weeded annually and damaged or discarded materials replaced if desirable. To avoid playing the "numbers game" (in which a motley collection of unused materials takes up space simply for the purpose of having enough items to meet standards) funds must be allocated not only for replacement of materials but for improvement and updating of the collection. As innovations in the field of educational media continue, funds must be made available for new programs. A recent innovation in the elementary school

Eureka! A Staff of Twelve

media center is children's books on microfiche. The advantages of such a program are obvious. Since space is at a premium in most elementary school media centers, the addition of books on microfiche at a low cost will enable the center to add a considerable amount of research material without having to cope with the problem of storage. If no provision has been made for the addition of new equipment and materials, the program will remain static.

Finally, long-range planning and preparation of budget needs should always be directly related to program areas and services. Taxpayers have a right to know what educational outcomes might be expected given increased expenditures in specific areas. The following sample budget does relate cost estimates for staff, facilities, equipment, and instructional resources directly to services. It was prepared for the Ferguson-Florissant (Missouri) School District under the direction of Media Coordinator John Bizzell and Director of Library Services, Stella Farley. It is reprinted here with permission and is prefaced by the following statement from Mrs. Farley:

> The pattern for staffing was developed to meet minimum standards set for school libraries in the State of Missouri. Experience has proven that the most effective media, library programs, those truly meeting the needs of students, are found in the schools where a professional media/librarian is stationed. It is our goal, therefore, to increase the number of professionals as budget permits until each school media center is directed by a certificated media librarian.

A Plan for Media Center Development

Staff	Cost	Student Use	
1 Media librarian per 2200 students	$ _____	A. Recreational reading B. Limited research C. Scheduled class visits under supervision of teacher D. Organization of materials & student accessibility	*First year of the program*
1 Media specialist for 17 schools	$ _____		
1 District Media Coordinator	$ _____		
1 full time aide	$ _____		
3 part time aides	$ _____		

	Staff	Cost	Student Use
(cont.) *First year of the program*	Mother volunteers (approx. 200-untrained) ESEA Title III assistance 1 media center clerk	$ _____ $ _____ $ _____	
Second year of the program	1 media librarian per 1500 students (4 schools) 1 media library aide & 3 part time media aides 1 media specialists for 17 schools Mother volunteers (approx. 200-untrained) 1 District Library Supervisor 1 District Media Coordinator 1 media center clerk (6 hrs. a day)	$ _____ $ _____ $ _____ $ _____ $ _____ $ _____ $ _____	A. Recreational reading B. Limited research C. Scheduled class visits under supervision of classroom teacher D. Some flexible scheduling E. Some independent study F. Summer library program-2 schools
Third year of the program	1 media librarian per 1000 students 3 media library aides in district 1 media specialist 1 District Library Supervisor 1 District Media Coordinator	$ _____ $ _____ $ _____ $ _____ $ _____	A. Recreational reading B. Assistance to students with research C. Classroom visits for library instruction D. Flexible scheduling
	1 library clerk 1 graphic artist 1 media center clerk (6 hrs.) Mother volunteers	$ _____ $ _____ $ _____ $ _____	E. Independent study F. Group projects G. Guidance in listening and viewing activities H. Personal and social guidance (limited) I. Reading guidance J. Use of large variety of materials at school K. Organized use of library skills unipac L. One school introduction of learning center concept

Eureka! A Staff of Twelve

Staff	Cost		
1 media/librarian per 500 students (5 in district)	$ _____	Repeat of A thru L under third year Student use. M. Use of curriculum learning package teaching library skills through the social studies N. Use of games, puzzles in teaching library skills O. Planning for learning center concept use in several schools	*Fourth year of the program*
1 media aide in 12 schools	$ _____		
1 media specialist for 17 schools	$ _____		
1 District library Director	$ _____		
1 District Media Director	$ _____		
1 graphic artist	$ _____		
1 media center clerk (6 hrs.)	$ _____		
Mother volunteers	$ _____		
1 library clerk (20 hrs. per wk.)	$ _____		
1 media/librarian per 500 students (5)	$ _____	Refinement of Fourth year activities A-M. N. Learning center concept beginning in all schools O. Profiles of children's activities to assist teacher diagnosis and prescription for individualized teaching P. Accessibility of materials much greater through better cataloging and inventory Q. Book and media talks expansion R. Visual literacy and filming emphasis	*Fifth year of the program*
1 media/library aide in each school (17-5 additional)	$ _____		
2 media specialist—1 for 8 schools, 1 for 9	$ _____		
work-study students from junior colleges	$ _____		
1 District Library Director	$ _____		
1 District Media Director	$ _____		
1 graphic artist (District)	$ _____		
1 media center clerk (6 hrs.)	$ _____		
1 library clerk (40 hrs. per wk.)	$ _____		

Services

1. Surveyed libraries
2. Developed procedures manual, philosophy, objectives and selection policy.
3. Weeded and reorganized existing collections.
4. Trained volunteer help and supervised processing.
5. Found and listed all media material in book catalog for eventual cataloging.

First year

6. Selected pre-processed materials for libraries and planned for a balanced collection.
7. Planned and projected needs as to staff, facilities, equipment and collection.
8. Planned cooperatively with secondary librarians for a district centralized ordering and processing center under the supervision of the District Library Supervisor.
9. Developed and distributed informational bulletins to staff.
10. Service to teachers *by request only.*

Second year

Reviewed selected topics above and refined
1. Expanded services to teachers.
    a. Answered teacher requests.
    b. Prepared resource units.
    c. Planned effective instruction in use of library.
    d. Helped in selection of materials for classes.
    e. Gave reference service to teachers.
2. Initiated service to students.
    a. Stimulated and encouraged interest in recreational reading.
    b. Reading guidance in cooperation with classroom teacher.
    c. Storytelling and book talks.
    d. Instruction in library skills.
3. Print production facility expanded to district use.
4. Audio tape duplication begun for district personnel.
5. Lamination of materials for teachers.
6. Loan of specialized equipment from Media Center.
7. Initiated unified media order.
8. Beginning of unification of professional library materials.
9. Master card catalog file beginning.

Third year

Continued expansion of above services plus:
1. Graphic arts service initiated.
2. Centralized processing of elementary and Title II materials begun.
3. Centralized cataloging of materials purchased on unified orders.
4. Study Trip handbook developed.
5. Literature appreciation program begun.
6. Participation of librarians and aides on curriculum committees with principals, consultants and other staff.
7. In-service workshops for teachers.
8. Development of learning center concept.
9. Developed handbook of audiovisual materials.
10. Initiated order for batteries and bulbs for all elementary schools.
11. Developed and distributed Copy Center guidelines.
12. Expanded electronic equipment repair service to include all language labs, TV distribution systems, television receivers, sound systems and all A/V equipment.

Eureka! A Staff of Twelve

13. Labeling system for audiovisual equipment initiated.
14. Initiated district office equipment repair service.
15. Added cameras, sound system with 4 microphones and mic mixer, slide dissolve unit, slide/sound tape recorder to equipment for loan from Media Center.

1. In-service workshop for library assistants and volunteers.
2. Increased in-service for librarians.
    A. District in-service participation
        (1) Multi-media learning.
        (2) Learning to Learn skills materials
    B. Summer Projects-2 schools
    C. Special In-service programs for media librarians:
        (1) Update information in Children's Literature
        (2) Reading levels—Reading consultant
        (3) Human relations
    D. Participation of librarians and library assistants in faculty meetings and orientation of teachers services and materials available.
3. Definition of role of Media Librarian and Library Assistant. Gradual evolution.
4. Evaluation of new materials by all media personnel through special assignments.
5. Developed library skills through the Social Studies unipacs.
6. Learning center concept planned for other libraries.
7. Availability and expansion of professional materials and services to teachers.
8. Survey of summer library programs.
9. Continued effort in literature appreciation program.
10. Resource file developed.
11. Improve district slide collection.
12. Revision of Copy Center guidelines (Graphic Communication Handbook—August 1972)
13. Communication Workshop
14. Developed and distributed Transparency Master Booklet.
15. Initiated microfilming service—business records, student records, personnel records.
16. Employ work study students to provide more district media services. Media production, graphics, copy center, electronic equipment repair and processing materials.
17. Expand office equipment repair service to include typewriters.
18. Switch from federal support of graphic artist to district support.
19. Develop request system for standard school forms through the District Copy Center.
20. Develop systems for accounting for cost of media production services for better accountability.

Fourth year

Fifth year

1. Emphasis on mother volunteer recruitment and training to further implement learning center concept in all libraries.
2. Emphasis on team effort—librarian, library assistant, consultant—to make the library center of the school program and to increase accessibility of materials and services to students and staff.
3. Schools wired for cable television reception.
4. District television studio equipped for cable transmission from studio to schools or community subscribers.
5. Revise study trip handbook for elementary staff members.
6. Pilot program—Use of computer in elementary schools.
   A. Develop curriculum for intermediate grade levels.
   B. Use in instructional program with math or spelling.
   C. Purchase used computer or lease computer time through a terminal.
7. Develop mediated alternative school for handicapped or homebound students.
   A. Cassette and other learning materials circulation.
   B. Two-way conference telephone.
   C. Cable television.
8. Increased production of media such as Super 8mm film loops and sound slide units.
   A. Science
   B. Physical Education
   C. Art
   D. Use and production of media hand made slides photography
9. Develop visual literacy curriculum.
10. Improve elementary school newspapers.
11. Improve and expand copy, duplication, and print services for all schools and offices.

Facilities & Equipment

First year

A. Facilities—Some inadequate because of insufficient space, physical conditions (lighting, sound control), and multi-use of space.
B. Equipment—Inadequate especially for small group and individual use.
A. Facilities
   1. Establish district centralized media processing center.
   2. School libraries
      a. Space—begin to attain following minimum standards.
         1. Reading area—min. area 25 sq. ft. per student for 45 students or 10% of enrollment (whichever is larger)

Eureka! A Staff of Twelve

      2. Workroom-storage area, 400 sq. ft.
      3. Media equipment, 400 sq. ft.
      4. Viewing & Listening, 800 sq. ft.
      5. Conference Room, 120 sq. ft.
      6. Professional Library & Workroom, 400 sq. ft.
    b. Physical Conditions—begin to attain the following physical improvements:
      1. Adequate light, heat, ventilation, & air conditioning.
      2. Electrical Service—duplex outlets in each wall of reading room, equipment area, and office conference room. Multiple strip molding in workroom and viewing and listening area.
      3. Floor covering—noise and glare reducing materials.
      4. Ceiling—accoustically treated.
      5. Draperies—selected in terms of lighting requirements and artistic decoration.
B. Equipment and Furniture—begin to attain ALA-DAVI standards.
    1. Shelving—meets dimensional standards, adjustable.
    2. Tables & Chairs—proper height for group served, attractively designed and sturdily constructed. 10% of seating space devoted to carrels.
    3. Circulation desk—simple and functional. Height suitable for elementary student use.
    4. Card catalog cabinet, book trucks, legal size, filing cabinets, dictionary stands, atlas stands, large picture files, *typewriters*, wall glass exhibit case, informal furniture, art objects.
A. Improve and expand existing facilities as needed.

Library Resources

A. The budget for library materials should be increased from the present level of support to $_____ per student for the following reasons:
    1. Materials centers are including a wider variety of materials.
    2. Prices are constantly increasing.
    3. Newer curriculum developments and individualized instruction place much greater dependence on material resources.
B. It is the concensus of the media group; that the district collection of instructional materials should be expanded to include a wider range of materials which normally are relatively expensive for individual school purchases in terms of actual capital outlay and time used. District purchase could be justified for these types of materials where it would be difficult to justify

purchase for an individual school. In building a district collection of these materials the large accessibility of titles should more than offset the sacrifice that will be made in terms of immediacy of use.

These materials would be distributed on request from the A/V department much as the district filmstrip collection has been done.

1. Film Loops-although rather new, this medium appears to possess potential for becoming an important part of individualized instruction.
    a.) It is recommended by the media group that all film loops presently in individual schools be sent to the District A/V Department to be available on request with other materials.
    b.) A budget of $_____ should be provided to purchase a selected library of loops. Approximately one hundred could be purchased for this sum, following an average cost of $_____ each.
2. Filmstrips and slides—While it may be desirable to have a basic collection in individual schools, the wider range of titles available through the district collection should prove more economical and ultimately more useful.
    Recommendation: The District Collection should be expanded to include many of the newer titles in science, social studies, and language skills. Approximately two hundred titles could be added for $_____.
3. Prepared Transparencies and Manipulative Devices for Overhead Projection—These materials of a specialized nature would fill a definite need on a district-wide basis. Examples of materials in this category are: a working model of a 4-cylinder engine, abacus, prepared transparencies for topics such as Oceanography, etc.
    Recommendation: $_____ for acquisition.
4. Transparency Originals—(Packets from 3M Company)—These packets which pertain to the elementary level should be purchased and housed at the A/V Department. Individual schools or teachers would receive a listing of packets and could then request them for selection of those appropriate to be made into transparencies for their own school.
    Recommendation: Principals should send packets now available in their school to the A/V Department in order to avoid costly and needless duplication. $_____ would be sufficient to round out the collection.
5. Miscellaneous Media—(Three dimensional models and manipulative devices such as Apollo Space Craft, land form models, demonstration motors, etc.)
    Recommendation: $_____ budgeted to allow a variety of

Eureka! A Staff of Twelve

materials to be added to the collection.
Suggestions from teachers for materials for acquisition will be appreciated and considered.
6. Materials to be located in each library/media center are: *See chart on next page.*

Equipment

Instructional Equipment: As a basic minimum School Board funds should be budgeted to match anticipated NDEA Title III funds. If such grant funds are not available a greater district effort will be necessary to keep pace with rapidly expanding educational technology.

A. A central Elementary Production Center should be equipped with the following:
   1. A commercial Dry Mount Press for laminating pictures, posters, etc. Cost—$ _____
   2. A photographic copy stand
      Cost—$ _____
   3. A macrozoom 35mm camera to use with the copystand.
      Cost—$ _____
   4. A Cassette Tape Duplicator
      Cost—$ _____
   5. Mimeograph Machine $ _____
   6. Thermofax Copier $ _____
   7. Spirit Duplicator $ _____
   8. Stencil Light Board $ _____
B. Equipment with video recorder systems including:
   1. Video Camera ensemble $ _____
   2. Video recorder $ _____
   3. Video Monitor $ _____
   4. Video Camera Viewfinder $ _____
   5. Zoom lens $ _____
C. Each elementary school should be provided with at least one:
   1. Carousel Slide Projector $ _____
   2. Language Master or Card Reader $ _____
D. Central T.V. Distribution Systems should be installed in schools that do not have them and need them. They are:
   Approximate Cost $ _____
E. Within each school, each team of teachers should have as a basic minimum:
   1. A reel-to-reel tape recorder $ _____
   2. An overhead projector $ _____
   3. A filmstrip projector $ _____
   4. 16mm projector $ _____

Materials

Materials	Number required to meet standards	Number on Hand	Number Needed	Cost to meet standards
Books				
Periodicals				
Newspapers				
Filmstrips				
Recordings				
Slides				
Art Prints				
Other graphics				
Study prints				
Globes				
Maps				
Microfilm				
Transparencies				
Realia				
Other				

F. Each teacher in most cases should have as a minimum:
    1. One record player$ _____
  2. One listening system consisting of 8 headphones and jack strip$ _____
    3. One filmstrip previewer$ _____
G. Each materials center should be provided with:
    1. Typewriter$ _____
    2. Paper cutter$ _____
    3. Stapler$ _____

Enter Uncle Sam

Uncle Sam probably should receive more credit than any other person, school district or agency for the increase in elementary school library supervisors in this country since 1965. With the advent of the Elementary and Secondary Education Act, already overworked school administrators surveyed with dismay the mountain of paperwork required to qualify for federal funds under Titles I, II, or III, and immediately appointed a district wide (or in many instances an elementary) library/media supervisor. Admittedly, the paperwork over the years since 1965 has decreased but not to the point where a considerable amount of time annually is not required.

Initially in the federal program, librarians were convinced that the individual responsible for dreaming up the required paperwork to qualify for funds under Title II of the Act must have harbored in his subconscious a traumatic experience with a school librarian which led to a deep-seated desire to get even with same.

Step One on the road to federal funds was a monstrous form called, EVALUATION DATA. This form required the library supervisor to inventory *every* item in the elementary schools and to supply the following information:

1. Library Books, broken down by classification area.
   Number of different titles, number of volumes, number of titles copyrighted within the last five years and a numerical evaluation of how adequate each classification is for instructional needs.

2. Periodicals. Broken down into 30 subject categories.
   Periodicals were to be rated according to those which included

general coverage and pertinent to the instructional program, those appropriate for the educational level, those which met pupil needs and interests, and those which met faculty needs.

3. Other printed library materials, including pamphlets, documents, musical scores and supplementary texts.

> Information required included the number of titles copyrighted in the last five years, and a numerical instructional rating for each category.

4. Audio visual materials, including motion pictures, filmstrips, slides, transparencies, disc and tape recordings, picture sets, maps, globes, charts, others.

> Required here was the number of titles owned by the district in each category, and the number borrowed from outside sources.

5. Textbooks in every subject area.

> Again required was the number of titles, the number of copies and the number of titles copyrighted in the last five years with numerical instructional rating.

Once this inventory has been completed, the **PROJECT APPLICATION** was to be completed. This included the allocation data, the request for funds, and a complete breakdown of how funds were to be spent. Funds were allocated on a per-pupil basis in each school. Thus, assuming that a school was allocated one thousand dollars to spend for school library resources, the librarian, after preparing the order, also had to complete a form which required her to break down the order by print and non-print materials and determine the exact portion of funds to be spent for each type of item within each Dewey subject category.

Several weeks (or sometimes months) after forms were completed and sent to the State Department of Education for approval, the message was received from the department indicating that orders could be sent.

One factor which complicates the spending of federal funds somewhat to this day is the cut-off date (usually June 30) after which no additional orders may be placed. In theory, this should not prove to be a problem. Congress is supposed to appropriate the funds soon after the beginning of the fiscal year (July 1). If (in theory) funds are received in a school district early in the fall, all orders should be placed, short shipments reordered, and

Uncle Sam Hates Library Supervisors

invoices paid long before June 30. However, if, as has frequently happened, Congress does not release the funds until March and the school districts cannot begin ordering until April or May, the situation becomes complicated. For example, if a thousand dollar order placed in May, arrives three hundred dollars short after June 30, the three hundred dollars cannot be spent but must be returned to the government, who, in turn (since funds were returned) assumes that funds are not needed and may cut the district's allocation for the next year.

Any librarian or library supervisor who has come this far along the bureaucratic road is not about to return funds that have been so toilsomely earned. Thus, being a rather ingenious group as a whole, several solutions to the problem have been found. The most common solution is to over-order, placing a money limit beyond which the company should not go. Most jobbers recommend an over-order of twenty percent but the experienced supervisor has found that increasing the order by fifty percent does not always guarantee full delivery. To really beat the odds, ordering twice the amount that funds will cover is the safest approach.

Another approach is to keep in contact with a local dealer; by warning him that by mid-June you may have extra funds to be expended quickly, he may well increase his stock on hand to take advantage of this unexpected windfall. The librarian can then visit the dealer's showroom and make her selections from personal examination or have the dealer bring sample materials to the district for this purpose. A recent change in the law has allievated this problem somewhat.

Uncle Sam Brings the Sisters

Federal programs under ESEA apply to children in the private schools as well as the public schools of a district. Therefore, the library supervisor is given the added responsibility for the ordering, processing, and record keeping for all materials sent to the private schools. This requires a close working relationship with the staff of those schools, many of whom are Sisters who may feel that if you ignore a Federal form long enough, it will go away. One supervisor has discovered that the good Sisters are possibly the most democratic of all school administrators. Given a federal allocation of $650 for a school with twenty classrooms, each classroom will receive $32.50 to use in ordering materials for the school library. And each teacher, wanting to spend her $32.50 wisely, searches every catalog she can get her hands on, making notes on scraps of paper or the backs of envelopes. When the principal presents the library supervisor with this unorthodox array of "orders", the supervisor discovers that:

1. The $650 allocation has been spread over eighty-four companies.
2. Titles of items have been given without additional bibliographic data.
3. Company names may be included but no addresses.
4. Much material has been ordered (i.e. thumbtacks, erasers, etc.) that does not qualify as library resources.

Attempting to reach the principal to bring order to this chaos is no easy matter. Most of the private school principals teach a class as well, and while phones may ring, and fire, flood, and famine abound, the library supervisor learns very quickly that "Sister cannot be disturbed while she is teaching her class." However with patience, a bit of good humor and a measure of cooperation, the problems can generally be straightened out.

The Special Grant: For Those Who Are Brave Enough to Apply

Special grants for school district library/media services are available under a number of government and nongovernmental programs. Most states set aside a portion of Title II ESEA monies for the purpose of taking care of special needs in a school district. In addition, Title III of the Elementary and Secondary Education Act allows funds for innovative programs designed to upgrade educational opportunities for disadvantaged students. Recently, Title III of the ESEA has been combined with Title III of the National Defense Education Act which provides funds on a matching basis for the purchase of audiovisual equipment. While state departments of education set forth guidelines for special needs applications under ESEA II, project proposals for ESEA III usually are approved by Federal rather than State offices. Each school district in a State is eligible to apply for special needs or Title III grants for any individual public or private school within the district. The statistical portion of the application is similar to the allocation data cited earlier. But in addition to detailing statistically exactly how funds are to be spent for the project, a written explanation must be included which details the need and how the need might be met (and evaluated) if additional funds are forthcoming.

One example of an outstanding ESEA Title III Program is the "Multi-Media Approach to Learning" program of the School District of Greenville County in Greenville, South Carolina. Betty Martin, Media Services Consultant, describes the program as follows:

The Multi-Media Approach to Learning at the Greenville Middle School

This program has two primary objectives: improving each student's attitude toward learning, and raising students' achievement in the four main academic areas.

The project emphasizes the exploration of varying teaching methods, supported by multi-media. Both print and non-print media are utilized extensively.

Originally funded in 1970 as a PL 89-10 Title III Project, the program is now funded by the local school district.

During its four years of operation, the project has become an integral part of the instructional program of the Greenville Middle School. Teachers and staff at the school work closely with the project staff to maintain the most desirable learning conditions.

The program's four main thrusts are:
1. Developing more positive student self-concepts. This is done by providing
   A. Opportunities for Student Success
      The students' abilities and needs are assessed, and they are provided materials and learning activities which will insure success. Students are also given options in ways of learning which are most productive for them.
   B. Warm Student-Teacher Relationships
      Teachers talk with students about their concerns, enjoy informal contacts with them and strive to foster a friendly understanding with them. An openness to social and academic

learning has come as a result of knowing that teachers care about the students.
C. Development of Student Leadership
Opportunities for student leadership are provided in small group work, where a student serves as chairman. Student participation in the speakers' program and tutoring program, and service in the media center, promote self-direction and training in leadership.

2. Using Varied Instructional Media and Methods
   A. Individualized Instruction
   The student and his individual needs have become one of the project's most important considerations. There are several methods used to individualize the instruction. These methods include commercially prepared materials, teacher-prepared learning packages or 'contracts', individual learning centers and independent studies.
   B. Team Teaching
   One type of cooperative teaching which has been utilized in the project is an interdisciplinary team composed of one teacher from each of the four main subject areas. Students are grouped and regrouped within their units, depending upon the purposes of instruction.
   C. Small Group Work
   While some of the teachers have chosen to utilize these methods, others have explored the use of small group work and educational games. NO single teaching method has been adopted by all teachers. Project plans give students and teachers the option of choosing a variety of ways in which to learn.
   D. Open, Accessible Media Center
   In support of all teaching methods, the availability of an open, accessible media center and an adequate media staff is crucial. Students, individually, in small groups and as whole classes, use the media center's resources when the need arises. All media and equipment is circulated to students and teachers.

3. Student Involvement
   A. Planning
   Students are active participants in the learning process. Individuals or groups of students and their teachers plan units of work, contracts and other learning activities. This planning includes identification of objectives and methods and evaluation and selection of media.
   B. Selection
   Students choose to use the media which is most suitable for their style of learning. The variety of available resources

include filmstrips, 8mm loops, disc recordings, transparencies, slides, audio and video tapes, books, magazines, pamphlets, and instructional television.

C. Construction of Media

Students find most stimulating the construction of original media. To share their research and personal interest with other students, they develop and construct slide sequences, 8mm films, still photographs, transparencies, filmstrips, audio and video tapes, and/or combinations of these media.

D. Tutoring

Seventh and eighth grade students are involved in tutoring students in their peer group and in elementary grades. Growth is noted both in the academic areas and in social relationships, for the tutors and the tutees.

E. Evaluation

Students often evaluate their own progress informally. In addition, students discuss with teachers their progress toward achieving individual objectives. Often this report is shared with parents.

4. Community Resources

A. Field Trips

Trips into the community are planned for teams, whole classes and small groups, so that students may learn from observing governmental, industrial or business activities, or educational institutions.

B. Interviews

Students may go to interview a person in the community who has had much training and experience in a particular area. Interviews might be filmed or taped and shared with other students.

C. Parent Volunteers

Volunteer parents perform a number of valuable services for the schools. Parents serve as clerical helpers, media center aides and instructional aides, and help provide transportation for field trips. After initial training sessions, parents give many hours to tutoring individual students.

D. Speakers, Programs

Students and teachers have had opportunities to participate in a continuing program of speakers from the community. Knowledgeable adults are invited to the school to discuss a variety of high interest and/or curriculum related topics selected by the students and teachers. Among other sources, the school district's Community Resources File has been used to identify interesting and informative speakers."

As one can see from the foregoing description, any application or request for funds for a particular program must be preceded by carefully developed performance goals and objectives. It is no longer enough to equate increased expenditures with increased educational output. In this age of accountability, expected educational achievement on the part of students must be carefully projected and instruments for measuring the expected performance of students within a particular area must be developed. In addition, the library supervisor who attempts budget development, whether for a federal grant, private foundation grant, or based on the general instructional materials funds of the district, must have the greatest possible input from the users of the services and materials in order for funds to be expended wisely. Only when services are clearly defined, can facilities, staff and materials be added which will best provide for the needs of students and teachers.

Titles Mentioned in this Chapter

A Manual on Certification Requirements for School Personnel in the USA. NEA. 1971.

"A Plan for Media Center Development" by John Bizzell and Stella Farley. Ferguson-Florissant School Dist. St. Louis County, Mo. 1974.

"A Multi-Media Approach to Learning at the Greenville Middle School" by Betty Martin. Brochure of the Greenville (Ky) School District. 1974.

5

All This and the Censors Too!
or Life in a Conservative Community

Library literature abounds with academic treatises on censorship and intellectual freedom. In theory, intellectual freedom is to be preserved at all costs. In practice, librarians are accused of lacking the guts to order controversial materials or of purchasing materials which might prove objectionable to one group or another, and hiding them under the counter. In case after case, public and school librarians who have placed the value of intellectual freedom above their need for a paycheck have found themselves without a job. When academic theory meets community reality, something has to give as is illustrated by the following set of circumstances which occured recently in a mid-western state.

The Censor at Work
In the early 1970s a school librarian from a small town in the Midwest wrote a letter. The letter was to have repercussions not only for her but for the entire community in which she lived. It was written to a local newspaper, and in the letter the librarian defended the right of a group of high school students to write, publish, and distribute a newspaper which expressed views not only contrary to the administration of the school but to the mores of the community. While her letter did not necessarily place a stamp of approval on the contents of the student paper, it did

uphold the right of the students to express their views. In the uproar that followed, the librarian was asked for her resignation. She took her case to the local Library Association's Intellectual Freedom Committee which concluded after an extensive investigation that the Library Bill of Rights had, indeed, been violated. This did not, however, get her job back, and the librarian was left to seek a position in another school district. The repercussions of this incident were many.

1. A group of local parents proceeded with an investigation of instructional materials found in the school district (knowing full well that their children could not have learned the unorthodox views expressed in the newspaper at home!)

2. This same group of "concerned" citizens began a careful examination of the holdings of the public library in the town and concluded that all materials deemed by them to be subversive, or by authors considered by them to be subversive, should be so marked.

3. The Director of the Public Library stood firm against such labeling and was supported by the Library Board.

4. The following year, changes in the library personnel and in the personnel of the Library Board occured. Pressure from the right wing element of the community on the County Court which appointed board members caused a majority of new appointees to be those who held ultra-conservative views. The first action of the newly organized Board was to ask for the resignation of the Library's Director. This resignation was rapidly followed by the resignation of all professional staff members who resigned in support of the Director's stand on intellectual freedom.

5. A small community group of those supporting intellectual freedom was formed to protest against the removal of the Director. Members of this group began attending meetings of the Board, serving as a "watchdog" committee to ascertain any form of censorship which might be proposed.

6. Meanwhile, back in the schools, the earlier mentioned "concerned citizens" group examined and loudly protested against textbooks used in the secondary social studies programs, forcing the School Board to offer alternative texts.

7. This same group prevented a lecture on UFOs in high school science classes and began examination of the supplementary and library materials used by students in the district.

To date, the local School Board spends a good deal of its time hearing complaints about materials used in the schools. All librarians who were forced to resign have relocated in other parts of the country and the community remains divided into three elements: (1) The conservative element, ready to protest against materials found in the public library or the schools at the least provocation; (2) the small group concerned with intellectual freedom; (3) the vast majority of citizens who don't give a damn.

In an effort to awaken the apathetic majority, three citizens, including a library supervisor, an English teacher and a college student researched the problem of intellectual freedom and prepared a three part series which was offered to, and rejected by, local newspapers. Hope for the community does, however, lie in the efforts of the "Watchdog" committee which continues to keep a sharp eye on library collections to see that all views are represented and whose members faithfully attend the meetings of the Library Board in an attempt to maintain a semblance of intellectual freedom in the community.

Living in a Community of Censors

The foregoing situation is recounted here to give the reader some idea of the problems that will be encountered by librarians who are caught in such a wave of censorship hysteria. School district selection policies, basically designed to handle the complaint of the occasional concerned parent, have not been able to withstand the onslaught of organized groups whose carefully planned attacks on both school and public libraries are frequently successful.

The reason for the success lies in the apathy of most citizens toward the issue of intellectual freedom. Organized groups (usually right wing) who are determined to "safeguard the morals of our young" periodically receive from their national headquarters bibliographies of materials considered by the powers-that-be to be subversive or of questionable moral quality for use by young people. Through petition, formal complaint, and often with the help of the press, the issue is brought before the school board. Petitioners loudly denounce administrators, teachers and librarians for placing in the hands of children materials of questionable worth. If their requests for removal of materials are granted, the librarian or library supervisor is left with two choices: (1) buy only the noncontroversial since students' minds should remain asleep rather than challenged, or (2) look for a job in a less conservative community. Those who would urge a third option (stay and fight) as the only option open to the librarian have forgotten the apathetic majority in the community. Only when the apathy is overcome can such a fight be successful.

Censorship and the Elementary Library Supervisor
Even those who are most verbal in their cry for intellectual freedom in the secondary and public libraries will on occasion voice some reservations about materials considered suitable for elementary school children. Few instances of censorship in the elementary school library have been brought to light, perhaps because elementary librarians have taken great care that no controversial materials find their way into the elementary library/ media center; or because few materials written on the first-through sixth-grade reading level in the past carried controversial overtones; or because it has never occured to anyone that objectionable material could possibly be found in an elementary materials center and thus, the censors have never bothered to look.

Admittedly, ten or even five years ago, materials selection on the elementary level was a fairly noncontroversial activity. The unwritten law of juvenile publishers prohibited "unsuitable" language or objectionable situations in children's books. As little as ten years ago, even those books written for older youngsters, which might be read by a precocious sixth grader, contained no problems much greater than "Will he take me to the

All This and the Censors Too!

Prom?" While this was considered advanced reading for sixth graders by some parents and teachers, still, moral values of the day were intact (as was the heroine's hymen) and no real objection was raised. Thus, for many years it has been relatively quiet on the elementary library front. Considering that few elementary libraries were in existence up until five years ago, it would be safe to say that the problem of censorship at this level has been practically nonexistent.

By now the new supervisor is possibly breathing a sigh of relief, feeling that with all of the problems involved in dealing with administrators, staff members, volunteers, teachers, students, bids, budgets, bureaucracy, and the host of other problems involved in her job, it is a relief to know that she is safe in the area of censorship. Not so!

In 1964, the unwritten law of publishers mentioned earlier was stretched a bit when Harper & Row brought out Louise Fitzhugh's *Harriet, the Spy*. In the book, Harriet emerges as a most unconventional child who pays little attention to her parents and delights in hiding and listening to conversations never meant for her ears. Aside from Harriet's colorful language (colorful in 1964 that is) i.e., "I'll be damned if I will go to dancing school," the book was a departure from the norm in that Harriet appeared to be far wiser than her bumbling parents and far more outspoken that most parents and teachers felt a child should be. This very funny book, which ten and eleven year olds loved, was frowned upon by many parents and teachers.

Fitzhugh again shocked the library and educational world with the publication of her *Bang, Bang, You're Dead* (Harper & Row, 1969). In this picture book for younger children, two groups of little boys hold a real battle for possession of a favorite hill. Graphic illustrations and quaint phrases such as "Up your nose," and "pukeface" raised a number of parent-teacher eyebrows.

In 1971 it was not unusual to find on shelves in the upper elementary school William H. Armstrong's *Sourland*, (Harper & Row 1971) a sequel to his Newbery Award winning *Sounder*. Included along with the colorful language of the sheriff (i.e., "God-damn," "bastard," and "son-of-a-bitch") is the gang rape of a young black girl. While the incident is not graphically described, it does occur.

Among the 1972 offerings of juvenile publishers are Norma Klein's, *Mom the Wolf Man and Me* (Pantheon) and the Newbery Award winner, *Julie of the Wolves* by Jean George (Harper & Row). In the first book, Brett, an illegitimate child, questions her mother about the sexual relations between mother and her boyfriend, and brings mother and said boyfriend breakfast in bed on their wedding day. Sex again rears its head in *Julie*, when the half-wit boy to whom she has been married at age thirteen attempts to "mate" her.

These few illustrations should suffice to indicate the changing content of juvenile books. The burning question is no longer, "Will he take me to the prom?" but "If I go to the prom, will I need an abortion afterwards?"

The problems of selection for the library supervisor and for all elementary school librarians are obvious. While initial complaints concerning materials will most likely occur to the principal or librarian in the school, the supervisor is generally contacted if the complainant is not satisfied. Since the supervisor cannot possibly read and approve the 20,000 or so elementary books ordered each year for a medium-sized school district (nor should she), she must rely on the judgment of the professional staff. Selection meetings, a reading and recommendation or lack of same, by at least one member of the professional staff before materials are purchased, and a strong materials selection policy and procedure for handling complaints will considerably alleviate the problem.

Even these procedures, however, cannot totally keep a book from being removed from the shelves by a principal who would prefer to satisfy rather than fight a patron complaint. The procedure for filing an objection to a book can also be circumvented by the citizen who is allowed to speak for five minutes at the beginning of a School Board meeting. Many school boards hold this type of open meeting for citizen comments and complaints. While the Board is under no obligation to take action on the complaint or objection, the practice is questionable, since district personnel who might in some way be involved in the complaint have no opportunity to investigate or discuss the problem until after Board members and other interested citizens of the District have been given a one-sided view of it.

The emotional outbursts of such self-appointed censors who have the benefit of a full audience, are such that patrons leave such a meeting wondering if the public schools are, in reality, a part of a Communist plot to subvert the thinking of our youth, and debating whether or not the role of a public school teacher can be equated with that of a disciple of Satan himself!

Finally one must be aware of the attitude of many school administrators that "no book is so valuable that it cannot be replaced by another, if in doing so, one can avoid problems with the patrons of the school district." The librarian can fight this attitude only at the cost of her job. The library supervisor attempts to fight it through ongoing in-service education of both administrators and librarians through in-service meetings, memos, bulletins, recommended readings, and informal discussion. If education can overcome Victorian attitudes, it must be ongoing, relevant, and meaningful.

Problem Areas in Selection

The supervisor has a two-fold responsibility in the area of materials selection. While one of the major goals of the materials center is to provide materials on all sides of an issue to stimulate independent inquiry and the process of integrative reasoning, it is equally important to select the most objective materials possible to achieve a balanced collection. Those areas which provide special problems in selection include:

1. *Religion.* While most balanced collections do provide materials on many faiths, newer materials on witchcraft as a religion will be objected to by some groups.

2. *Social sciences.* No matter how objective the authors of books in this area may be, nor how well qualified they may be in their fields, right-wing groups will object to anything written by some well-known historians (Henry Commager, for example) and will object to any book which glorifies the United Nations

and government control of any part of our national life. Accounts of slavery (which may be factually true) may be objected to by Civil Rights groups, and treatment of any minority group often comes under criticism.

3. *Biography.* Again, right-wing groups will object to the inclusion of books on the lives of most Democratic Presidents, any authors considered to be radical, numerous newspaper men, or Communist leaders. They will press for inclusion in the collection books which glorify those that they consider to be true Americans.

4. *Science and applied science.* Books most in trouble in this area are those that have to do with animal and human reproduction. According to the censors, books on human anatomy which include the circulatory system, the digestive system, the nervous system, etc., are acceptable as long as we do not allow the child to know that he has a reproductive system. Also under fire in the science section are writings on evolution.

5. *Fine arts.* Books of famous paintings which include reproductions of nudes often receive complaints.

6. *Literature.* Few children's poets are considered to be radical enough for the censor's axe, with the exception of Langston Hughes. Censors may raise strong objections to the works of this fine poet being placed on the elementary school literature shelf.

7. *History.* Books which glorify the United States are acceptable. Those which criticize the United States in any way, or show the United States in an unfavorable light are objectionable.

Who Objects?

Among the most active special interest groups who seek to shape the minds of youth through control of reading materials are the following:

1. Right wing groups
2. Interests confined to the growth of industry and big business
3. Organized labor
4. Civil rights advocates

All this and the Censors Too!

5. Civil rights opponents
6. Women's liberationists
7. Fundamentalist religious groups
8. Consumer protection groups
9. Environmentalists, conservationists, animal lovers
10. Religious groups who object to population control.

A survey of titles included in the standard selection aid, *Books for Elementary School Libraries* (American Library Association 1969) reveals the following list of fairly standard acquisitions for the elementary library to which one or the other of the above group might object:

Title	Objecting Group	Reason for Objection
Linton, Ralph *Man's Way from Cave to Skyscraper* Harper 1947	7	Discusses evolution
Mead, Margaret *Anthropologists and What They Do* Watts 1965	1	author
Mead, Margaret *People and Places* World 1969	1	author
Joy, Charles R. *Race Between Food and People* Coward-McCann 1961	10	indicates that population growth is harmful
Jacobs, Lou *SST—Plane of Tomorrow* Golden Gate 1967	1,9	noise pollution government subsidy to business
Bergwin, Clyde *Animal Astronauts* Prentice-Hall 1963	9	experimentation with animals

Title	Objecting Group	Reason for Objection
Elting, Mary *We Are the Government* Doubleday 1967	1	includes a list of international organizations
Johnson, Gerald *Communism: An American's View* Morrow 1964	1	notes strength of Communism
Johnson, Gerald *The Supreme Court* Morrow 1962	1	shows influence of Court on lives of citizens
Sterne, Emma *I Have a Dream*	5	glorifies struggle for civil rights
Epstein, Edna *The United Stations* Watts 1966	1	considers the UN the first step to world government
Galt, Tom *How the United Nations Works* Crowell 1965	1	considers the UN the first step to world government
Sasek, M. *This is the United Nations* Macmillan 1968	1	considers the UN the first step to world government
Shippen, Katherine B. *The Pool of Knowledge: How the United Nations Share Their Skills* Harper 1965	1	considers the UN the first step to world government
Speiser, Jean *UNICEF and the World* Day 1965	1	considers the UN the first step to world government
Teltsch, Kathleen *Getting to Know the United Nations Peace Forces* Coward-McCann 1966	1	considers the UN the first step to world government

All This and the Censors Too!

Title	Objecting Group	Reason for Objection
Shippen, Katherine B. *Miracle in Motion: The Story of America's Industry* Harper 1955	2	discusses of need for government control of industry
Shippen, Katherine B. *This Union Cause* Harper 1958	2	shows organized labor in favorable light
Branley, Franklyn *The Earth: Planet Number Three* Crowell 1966	7	nonreligious explanation of the origin of the earth
Cooke, David C. *How Superhighways Are Made* Dodd 1958	9	does not detail the effects of highway building on environment
Bendick, Jeanne *The Shape of the Earth* Rand McNally 1965	7	describes evolution of earth in non-Biblical way
Lauber, Patricia *All About the Planet Earth* Random 1962	7	presents theories of evolution
Darling, Lois *The Science of Life* World 1961	1	discusses human reproduction
Frankel, Edward *DNA—Ladder of Life* McGraw-Hill 1964	7	discusses possibilities for creating life in test tube
Life *The Wonders of Life on Earth* Golden Pr. 1960	7	chapters on Darwin
Hyde, Margaret O. *This Crowded Planet* McGraw-Hill 1961	10	discusses problem of overpopulation

Title	Objecting Group	Reason for Objection
Zim, Herbert S. *Monkeys* Morrow 1955	7	points out similarity of monkey to man
Zim, Herbert S. *Golden Hamsters* Morrow 1951	1	illustrates and explains reproduction
DeSchweinitz, Karl *Growing Up: How We Became Alive, Are Born and Grow* Macmillan 1965	1	human reproduction
Gruenberg, Sidonie *The Wonderful Story of How You Were Born* Doubleday 1952	1	human reproduction
Epstein, Sam *The First Book of the World Health Organization* Watts 1964	1	world organization
Eberle, Irmengarde *Modern Medical Discoveries* Crowell 1968	7	machine substitutes for body organs
Hughes, Langston *The Dream Keeper and Other Poems* Knopf 1932	1	author
Hughes, Langston *Famous Negro Heroes of America* Dodd 1954	1 5	author and glorification of civil rights movement
Gregor, Arthur S. *Charles Darwin* Dutton 1966	7	explains Darwin's life and theories

Title	Objecting Group	Reason for Objection
Neyhart, Louise *Henry Ford: Engineer* Houghton 1950	3	glorifies industry
Selvin, David F. *Sam Gompers: Labor's Pioneer* Abelard-Schuman 1964	2	glorifies labor movement
Clayton, Ed *Martin Luther King: The Peaceful Warrier* Prentice-Hall 1964	5	fight to gain civil rights
Peare, Catherine Owens *The FDR Story* Crowell 1962	1	subject of biography
Beckhard, Arthur *Albert Einstein* Putnam 1959	1	subject of biography
Commanger, Henry Steele *The First Book of American History* Watts 1957	1	author and lack of glorification of U.S.
Catton, Bruce *This Hallowed Ground: The Story of the Union Side of the Civil War* Doubleday 1962	5	one sided account
Brink, Carol Ryrie *Caddie Woodlawn* Macmillan 1935	6	shows girl's tomboy antics as undesirable
Buck, Pearl S. *The Big Wave* Day 1948	1	author
Dahl, Roald *Charlie and the Chocolate Factory* Knopf 1964	4	workers in the story considered to be "slaves"

Title	Objecting Group	Reason for Objection
Graham, Lorenz *South Town* Follett 1955	5	racial problems sympathetically portrayed
Kipling, Rudyard *Just So Stories* Doubleday 1932	4	author
Lofting, Hugh *Doctor Dolittle* Lippincott 1967	4	considered by this group to be racist
Seredy, Kate *The Good Master* Viking 1935	6	tomboy becomes a gentle girl
Travers, Pamela *Mary Poppins Series* Harcourt 1934-35	4	considered racist
Twain, Mark *Adventures of Huckleberry Finn* Harper 1884	4	incident when Huck debates going to hell for saving a black man
Duvoisin, Roger *Petunia* Knopf 1950	6	female portrayed as silly goose

A sampling of more recent titles will show similar reasons for rejection by specific groups.

All This and the Censors Too!

Title	Objecting Group	Reason for Objection
Alderman, G. *Witchcraft in America* Four Winds 1974	7	discusses non-Christian beliefs
Anderson, Hans C. *The Woman with Eggs* Crown 1974	6	depicts a foolish woman
Katz, William *From the Progressive Era to the Great Depression* Watts 1974	1	U.S. not always shown in a favorable light
Mann, Peggy *Ralph Bunche: UN Peacemaker* Coward 1974	1	UN considered the first step to world government and control
Israel, Elaine *The Great Energy Search* Messner 1974	2	points up responsibility of industry in energy crisis
Wayne, Bennett *Black Crusaders for Freedom* Garrard 1974	5	praises Civil Rights movement
Olsen, James T. *Ralph Nader* Children's 1974	2	subject of the book

A Word on RE-Evaluation

The process of materials selection is a never-ending one. The impossibility of keeping up with the publishers' annual output in the juvenile book market, plus the added responsibility for the evaluation and selection of audiovisual materials would seem to indicate that materials selection is a full-time job. However, added to the problem of initial selection is the need for reevaluation of materials in existing collections.

In our changing society, children's books once considered classics have now found their way to the "no-no" list of one special interest group or another. The earlier list of materials which might come under fire from various special interest groups included six books long considered fairly standard acquisitions for elementary libraries. Two of the titles are former Newbery Award Winners. *Caddie Woodlawn* was considered in 1936 a charming book about a tomboy who (thankfully) grew up to be a young lady. Women's lib advocates would tell us today that this particular goal is not necessarily desirable and that young girls should not be "brainwashed" to think that it is.

The racist overtones of *The Voyages of Dr. Dolittle*, which won the award in 1923 were not objected to for forty years, yet today, many feel that *Dr. Dolittle* is a questionable choice for inclusion in the elementary materials center. While not a Newbery winner, it only took eight years for Dahl's *Charlie and the Chocolate Factory* to come under fire for the same reason.

A more recent award winner, William Steig's *Sylvester and the Magic Pebble* (Caldecott Award 1970), came under immediate fire from the Toledo, Ohio, Police Patrolman's Association, who protested the presence of the book in both school and public libraries. Their protest was supported by the large Toledo newspaper *The Blade*. whose editorial headline read, "A Book Shows Schools Bureaucratic Insensitivity" and by a local radio station, WSPD, who lauded the action of the school board in removing the book from the shelves.

It is essential then, for the library/media supervisor to keep abreast of current issues in the field of materials selection through professional reading and direct communication with others in the field. She should compile and issue lists of titles and areas which may call for closer evaluation before a decision to purchase is made. Questionable titles should be carefully screened by more than one member of the library/media staff, and if the decision is made to purchase, a file of pertinent information should be maintained for all questionable titles to provide justification for purchase, if necessary.

Mistakes Do Happen

While a number of school districts require materials for school libraries to be selected from specific lists, a number of others do not. When the former course is taken and extensive selection lists are compiled by teachers and librarians, mistakes in selection are not too likely to occur since each item added to the list has been reviewed by one or more responsible persons and has usually been well reviewed in library periodicals. While a "selection safety factor" is automatically built into such a list, many librarians find it restrictive since a new or highly desired item cannot be purchased until it is carefully reviewed and approved for the list, which is usually compiled once each year.

Other school districts have highly unrestrictive practices regarding the ordering of materials. The attitude taken by administrators is that librarians are trained in materials selection and through their work with teachers and pupils can best determine the needs in a specific school. Therefore, a selection list is superfluous and, in many cases, not in the best interests of a particular school. Librarians are given a free hand in ordering, with a final check of orders made by the library supervisor.

In this situation, the conscientious supervisor does make every effort to keep her staff members out of trouble through checking orders to see that they meet the district selection policy. However, being human, and being faced with the bulk of the orders each spring for numerous schools, the supervisor can not possibly check each order in detail and unsuitable materials do sometimes arrive. If the district has centralized processing, the questionable materials are likely to be caught there. If they are sent to the schools, it is hoped that the librarian in the school will take time to examine the new materials before preparing them for circulation.

A classic example of the kind of error which can occur has to do with the ordering and receipt for an elementary school library of an Ernest Hemingway recording which includes "Saturday Night in a Whorehouse in Billings, Montana." The circumstances were as follows:

1. The elementary librarian checked items in a record catalog that she wanted to order, not realizing that a secondary librarian

from whom she had borrowed the catalog had also checked several recordings.

2. The order was typed by the school clerk who was told to "type all checked items." Not noted for her powers of reasoning, she did exactly as told and typed, of course, the recording containing Hemingway's "Saturday Night in a Whorehouse."

3. The supervisor, faced with a stack of several hundred orders, and knowing from past experience that she could trust the judgment of this particular librarian, gave the orders a cursory glance and sent them on.

4. When the record arrived, the processing center secretary who checked the invoice left the item in question on the supervisor's desk with the following note: "I know relevance is 'in' these days, but how relevant can you get?"

The questionable material was forwarded to the High School English Department where it was put to good use.

Just as you supposedly can't tell a book by its cover, it is equally impossible to tell the contents of a filmstrip by its container. At present, the producers of audiovisual materials for the elementary school are "playing it as safe" as the book publishers did for many years. In an effort to produce something that will offend no one and because of the cost of AV materials production, the field is at the moment relatively free of controversial materials. However, there are signs of change and librarians will have to continue to evaluate each type of material as carefully as possible.

One additional problem which may arise in districts where selection lists are not used is in the area of teacher requests. Since the majority of teachers rarely make requests, the problem is usually confined to one or two teachers who have somewhat unorthodox approaches to their classes and consequently request materials which may be questionable in light of the district selection policy. One rather common problem is presented by the new sixth-grade language arts teacher who has recently completed studies of the great works of literature in college. Since she knows these works well, she feels these are the very things to which her eleven year olds should be exposed. An examination of the elementary library stacks reveals few, if any, of the works of Wolfe, Tolstoy, Faulkner, Steinbeck, etc., and she immediately demands these materials be ordered. Pointing out to her that the *Grapes of Wrath* is somewhat more than a beautiful story of migrant workers, or that some of the writers on her list used language a bit colorful for the elementary school, only serves to strengthen her resolve. The situation usually ends in a draw with the librarian ordering those classics which will do little more than bore eleven year olds, while at the same time suggesting more suitable materials that the teacher might want to consider for literature study.

Why should the librarian bother at all to order materials she feels are not entirely suitable for the materials center? The investment (providing the cost is low and the materials of some limited use) is not actually in the materials but in the future potential of the teacher. To turn a teacher completely off through disparaging her requests will result in the teacher "turning off" the library center as far as she and her pupils are concerned. The wise librarian knows that she can work with the teacher and her pupils and guide them toward more fruitful use of the library only if lines of communication are left open. Arbitrary censorship of teacher requests by the librarian, no matter how much such censorship may appear justified, may well result in the librarian having won a battle but lost the war. The moral is obvious. Teacher requests should be filled whenever possible with as little interference as is necessary from the librarian. Those who strongly disagree with this statement should ask themselves quite honestly if the materials center which they serve (and which is filled with what they consider to be entirely suitable materials) is as fully used by students and teachers as they would like it to be.

The supervisor who has worked to establish a district-wide elementary library/media program, organized volunteers, been a mother confessor to the professional staff, waded through the swamp of finances and federal programs, and fought the valiant battle with the censors, has one more task to accomplish. She must be able to determine if all of the time and effort expended by the library/media staff (and by herself) has been worthwhile in terms of improved educational opportunities for students. This means that an ongoing program of evaluation must be established and implemented.

6

The Fall from the Ivory Tower: The Supervisor as a Media Specialist

In this age of behavioral objectives and accountability, evaluation has become a dirty word among many educators. School librarians, who for years in their annual reports have evaluated library/media services by listing the number of new materials added during the year, the circulation carefully compiled by Dewey categories, the total number of student visits, and perhaps a description of any special activity which occurred during the year, are, to their dismay, now being asked exactly what these figures mean in terms of student achievement.

The supervisor who wraps herself in a cloak of authority and hibernates in the district's central office complex is equally guilty of attempting to evaluate the program through input factors rather than output or student achievement. It is very easy, when not on the firing line, for the supervisor to develop beautiful theories and utopian schemes and then to take the idealist position that "all of these plans for library activities and services will be effective because I say they are."

Most educators would concede that it is a major responsibility of the supervisor to develop plans for new materials and services which will hopefully increase the effectiveness of the library/media center in the school. But the effectiveness or lack of same of any new materials or program can best be determined if the supervisor accepts direct responsibility for their implementation. This means that she must be on the firing line (de-

The Fall from the Ivory Tower

fined as the school's instructional materials center) on a regularly scheduled basis working directly with teachers, students, and administrators to determine what actually happens when theory meets reality. The following examples should suffice to make this point.

Example One

Theory: If at any time the entire class makes use of instructional materials center facilities, the teacher should accompany and remain with the class.

Reality: A supervisor working in the school IMC discovered three variations on this theme in one afternoon. Teacher A did bring her class and remained with them (in body only) for the entire visit. However, Teacher A settled herself comfortably as far away from the students as she could get, whipped out her crossword puzzle book, and became absorbed in her hobby, taking time out to glare occasionally at a student who might indicate that he wanted her attention.

Teacher B, who always has fifty irons in the fire, turns on his "Mr. Charm" smile for the supervisor and assures her that he knows she won't mind if he leaves for a few minutes to take care of pressing business. His few minutes, of course, turn into the entire class period, leaving the supervisor with the choice of ignoring the policy or alienating the teacher if she attempts to enforce the policy.

Teacher C does accompany and remain with her class. She not only stays in the center but moves from child to child helping as help is needed. The problem arises when Teacher C (who wears very short skirts) leans over to assist a child. The view of her pink and blue underpants proves somewhat distracting to the fifth- and sixth-grade boys who are also working in the center and the supervisor wonders what kind of parent reaction there might be if youngsters happen to mention at the dinner table "that lady in the library with the fancy underpants."

Example Two

Theory: Library services should be broad in scope and meet the needs of the individual child.

Reality: To implement this theory, the supervisor encouraged display of small animals in the library. A kindergarten class beginning a unit on pets was invited to the center to view a live boa constrictor brought to school by its fourth-grade owner. While the five year olds gathered around, the proud owner allowed the snake to encircle her arm while she told the children about its feeding habits. The snake soon became as excited as the five year olds, and clamped its teeth on the fourth-grader's arm with no intention of letting go. The owner howled, the five year olds screamed, and the supervisor grabbed the nearest book and began clobbering the snake in an effort to release its grip. As the snake finally fell to the floor, pandemonium ensued. The frantic efforts of the supervisor, two teachers, the custodian, and the principal finally brought order to the chaos. The boa constrictor was returned to its cage and the now weeping owner was transported to the doctor for three stitches and a tetanus shot.

Example Three

Theory: Learning activities should be relevant to the learner and actual experience provided where possible.

Reality: A kindergarten class began a study of community helpers. Frequent visits to the library center were made to locate books, examine study prints, hear recordings, and view filmstrips on the topic. Storytime centered around the activities of the fireman, policeman, and postman. The supervisor made arrangements for the class to visit the post office and be given a tour. All went well on the visit as the postmaster explained the inner workings of the department in simple terms to the five year olds until one overly excited child lost his breakfast. This disturbing event was rapidly followed by two other children who viewed the mess and promptly lost their breakfasts as well, leaving the postal employees with a pungent atmosphere in which to work the rest of the day. A letter from the postmaster to the supervisor a few days later suggested that perhaps the concepts to be gained from a visit to the post office were a bit difficult for five year olds and in the future he would recommend that only children of nine years old or above make the visit!

Example Four

Theory: Primary children should be encouraged to undertake simple research projects.

Reality: Mrs. Adams, a second grade teacher, developed an independent study unit for her students on insects. Each child was given a simple question to answer and visited the IMC to listen, view, and read about insects. After each child presented the answer to his question, little Jerry noted that he had found additional information on the topic, which, of course, the teacher was delighted for him to present. This seven year old then informed the class that in order for the eggs of the polyphemus moth to hatch, the moth must first mate with another moth. "All animals," he stated "must mate to have young. Even (he continued) Mr. and Mrs. Adams must mate to have young." Mrs. Adams, who had paid little attention previously, to the research materials her students were using, quickly resolved to become more familiar with IMC materials in the future!

Example Five

Theory: Students should define and understand a problem before beginning a research activity.

Reality: The supervisor soon discovers that busy teachers frequently do not check to see that students understand research topics. Many librarians have been asked at one time or another for information on "the baseball song" (the Star Spangled Banner), the number of "countries" (counties) in a particular state, and the "continual shelf" (continental). The list is endless and the problem can be solved only through ongoing teacher training to get across the idea that simply because a teacher has stated a term or concept doesn't mean that the children understand it.

Example Six

Theory: Students should activly participate in work/study skills activities.

Reality: The "ivory tower" supervisor worked for months in developing a work/study skill manual for the primary grades. Page 3 of the manual contained a simple library citizenship story about a little girl who ran and yelled and played in the library and did not get her work finished. The story contained blank spaces where the children were to supply missing words. One sentence read, "She ran down the stairs, tripped and fell on her _____." When doing the story orally with a group of first graders, the supervisor discovered that the missing word most frequently supplied was "butt."

Page 8 of the manual required the junior researchers to look at a picture (which had the Dewey number of the topic underneath) and move to the shelves with that number to find a book about the topic pictured. The problem arose when thirty children all headed for the science stacks at the same time (since most of the topics pictured were in the 500 category). The page was quickly redone, using a number of categories to avoid the riot which took place the first time around.

The Fall from the Ivory Tower

Example Seven

Theory: Students should have access to all library materials.

Reality: This theory is valid only when the classroom teacher keeps a careful check on the activities of her students in the library/media center. The supervisor soon discovers that without close contact with the teacher on the expected activities of students many students will expend their energies studying the "dirty picture page" (usually the movie page) of the weekly periodicals, or viewing filmstrips when their assignment was a report on the structure of the atom.

Example Eight

Theory: Work/study skills lessons should be interesting, functional, and keep the attention of the student.

Reality: The elementary IMC had a seating capacity of 150 students. It was located on a lower level with an outside entrance. On one particular afternoon the center was full and the supervisor was working with twenty-five fourth graders on understanding the use of the atlas. To keep the attention of the twenty-five with so many other children in the center, she frequently asked for student participation in the lesson, watching each child carefully to see when he was ready to respond. A slight disturbance at one end of the center caught her attention and without looking up from her group, the supervisor admonished the disturbers to "keep the noise down" and went on with the class. When the period ended, the supervisor discovered from other teachers that the noise resulted from a teacher being knocked down by a couple of young seedy characters who had come into the building. As the lesson on the atlas continued, the young "hoods" were escorted from the center by two male teachers and turned over to the police.

Out of the Mouths of Babes

From among the many services and duties expected of the school library supervisor, evaluation does stand out in importance above all others. If a library/media center program is to grow, not only in those areas which can be measured quantitatively but in the quality of the programs and services offered, evaluation of each component of the program must be continuous and ongoing. While there are many forms of evaluation (and two excellent evaluative statements which relate staff, facilities and materials to service appear in the appendix) *students* are rarely consulted or asked to evaluate the instructional materials center program and services. The supervisor who really wants a frank and candid opinion of the effectiveness of the library or materials center would do well to sit down with students frequently and, with their permission, tape their responses to a few leading questions. The following is a sample of such an interview with five eleven-year-olds. While in some responses the students seemed to be attempting to impress the supervisor, answers for the most part were both candid and revealing, and provided a basis for evaluation that could be obtained in no other way.

Student IMC Evaluation

Interviewer: Suppose that I could wave a magic wand and the school library/media center would just disappear. Would it really make any difference to you in your learning?

Charles: If you can come to the library and look up this book on Cortez, it would save you a lot of time and trouble rather than having to go to the public library in the evening when you might not have enough time to go, and if you didn't get there you wouldn't have your work done.

Mike: I think it would make a lot of difference because sometimes kids can't work in the classroom because sometimes it's noisy and they need lots of things

The Fall from the Ivory Tower

	that will be down in the library and not in the classroom.
Judy:	I don't think you should take the library out because of all of the books they have for reference and homework. In our reading, we do essays and things and we come down here and we look in the books for the information that we need. It would make a lot of difference if they were to take it out.
Tim:	Well, if they took the library out, nobody could study about things like history, and as much money as they have spent on library materials, I'd say they really shouldn't take it out.
Interviewer:	Tim, you say that if the library were removed, no one could study. Couldn't you learn the same things from your textbooks?
Tim:	You couldn't learn as much.
Judy:	I think the library is for your own pleasure. Maybe you want to read a fiction book. It's fun to take your time and browse here in the school library.
Charles:	In reading we have to make essays and reports on certain things. I came down to the library to work on a report on the Pilgrims. I had to know the kind of clothes they wore and the way they acted when they came to Plymouth Rock.
Mike:	In history the teacher told us to use the encyclopedias and pick any time in history and get some facts on it, put it on note cards and make a report on it. I looked in the encyclopedias for the Pilgrims, and in the atlas to see where they landed. And if we didn't have these books, I couldn't do that.
Judy:	In science we've been using the reserve shelf. We can find books there that are not in the science part in the library, and the library has geographical dictionaries we use to look up maps and places, and

in the biographical dictionary you look for people, and we use the biography shelf in the library to look up the presidents and people like that and we look in other parts of the library for cooking and sewing and all kinds of books.

Tim: Well, in spelling we had to look up the presidents and I looked up Lincoln, that's how the almanac helped me, for looking up Lincoln, and I didn't get it, but anyway we had to write one hundred words and I found a few.

Interviewer: Boys and girls, how often do you come to the library? Do you have a regular weekly time when you come or do you use the library more often than once a week?

Charles: There are certain times during the week when the teacher brings the whole class, but we can come down alone any free time we get.

Tim: We come down on study periods or when we get free time. Mostly we study about what we have learned.

Mike: Usually during reading or science or history since we have different teachers for those, the teacher might say tomorrow we will work in the library and this way we've got another period there. I think the only day we don't come is Wednesday. That's a free reading period in our room. You have to have a book on Wednesday to read in the room.

Judy: On Mondays, our teacher makes us go to the library to get a book. Then in our free reading period on Wednesday if we don't have a book, he wants to know why not, since we were supposed to get one on Monday.

Interviewer: You have frequently mentioned books as part of your library activities. Do you use anything other than books?

The Fall from the Ivory Tower

Charles: I sometimes listen to records or tapes and look at filmstrips. There's a lot of stuff you can do besides reading books.

Mike: Sometimes when you see in the newspaper or on TV, that somebody has been shot or something important has happened, you can get more information from the newspapers or magazines in the library.

Tim: If you have a project on insects, for instance, you can listen to a tape with the headphones so you won't disturb anyone else. You don't always have to use the books. There are other things that tell just as much.

Interviewer: There are so many resources to use in getting answers to your questions or preparing reports, wouldn't it be easier if you could stay in your classroom and let your teacher simply tell you "who discovered this" or "who invented that?"

Mike: I'm not saying that a teacher's not smart, but there are some things he doesn't know that are in a book, and anyway, I like to find out for myself. Maybe he tells it a different way and when you read it, maybe you've got a different opinion about it so you should look it up for yourself and find your own facts.

Judy: Well, sometimes we have to go to the library to look things up because the teacher doesn't know the answer, or sometimes we do it because even if the teacher knows the answer he won't tell you. And besides I'd rather work in the library anyway because you can stand up and stretch and move around and there's lots more air. The classroom gets kind of stuffy sometimes.

Interviewer: Thank you, boys and girls.

A careful rereading of the foregoing interview will reveal not only student attitudes concerning library materials and services, but teacher practices and attitudes as well. Three of the major goals of this particular library/media program are:

1. To help students gain concepts independently through the use of a wide variety of carriers of knowledge
2. To develop on the part of students the skills needed for the successful independent pursuit of knowledge
3. To develop a love for reading and for books.

Student observations, at least in this instance, seem to indicate that this library center is well on the way to meeting its stated goals.

Students May Come and Students May Go but Statistics Go on Forever!

The earlier warning to the reader who might become involved in a new library/media program was to avoid making any more waves than necessary. In facing reality in the realm of evaluation, it is true that administrators expect a monthly or annual report filled with statistics and would immediately suspect the supervisor of not doing the job if she handed them a student tape in place of the revered statistical report. The new supervisor is then urged to include such a tape as a *part* of the annual report, for it does tell an important part of the library/media center story. In addition, statistics without interpretation are either meaningless or open to erroneous conclusions. If, for example, growth is shown in the size of the audiovisual collection, is growth also shown in the circulation of audiovisual materials?(If not, why not?) Are teacher requests greater or less than the year before? What accounts for the difference, if any? Are statistics currently being kept that are of no value?

The answers to these and many other questions raised by statistical reports can only be known firsthand if the supervisor stays out of her office as much as possible and gets into the schools.

Finally, if evaluation is to be realistic and valuable, it must be based on performance factors. In other words, the evaluative instrument must be preceded by a clear statement of program activities and purposes on which the evaluation is based.

Two evaluative statements appear in the appendix and contain specific criteria by which performance is to be measured.

A Final Word

The evaluation instruments in the appendix stress variety, flexibility, attractiveness, and receptiveness. While these attributes are applied to library/media center services and staff, they can be applied equally well to the school library supervisor. Her role encompasses not only work with students and teachers, but with patrons, administrators, other library/media personnel, and the community-at-large.

If the supervisor can keep both her sense of perspective and her sense of humor, the rewards of watching the library/media program grow to take its place as a truly effective educational force in the school, will far outweigh the frustrations.

The name of the game is HUMAN RELATIONS. One who lacks skill in dealing with others with courtesy, dignity, and respect will find the going difficult. Enthusiasm, combined with knowledge and sincerity and determination will go far in the successful development of a library/media program which will bring real meaning to the old cliche, "The library is the heart of the school." Perhaps a rewording of this cliche would be more appropriate, "Here in the school library/media center lies the heart of the library supervisor!"

Appendix

CRITERIA FOR EVALUATING RESEARCH CENTERS

Utica Community Schools
Reva Butson
Reprinted with permission of Charles Paine, Director of Audio and Visual Services, Utica Community Schools, Sterling Heights, Michigan.

The first objective of the school Research Center is to further the achievement of the overall objectives of the school. In addition, the school Research Center Teacher assumes the responsibility of formulating objectives that describe specific ways in which the school Research Center contributes to the growth of young people.

At least one cooperative classroom project (in which students help to select materials for the Research Center) should be presented during the school year. These projects tend to be presented in the language arts classes, but can be carried on in any part of the curriculum. Although the project is under the direction of the teacher and forms a part of the regular class work, the Research Center Teacher cooperates in every way possible and may be the one who motivates the teacher to include the project in the course. The students may concentrate on selecting books published during the current year, or they may evaluate a section of the Research Center's collection and recommend the purchase of books they feel the Research Center needs in that particular area. During the project, the students become acquainted with criteria for evaluating books and other materials and with the sources of information about materials.

Opportunity should be provided for the students to shape some Research Center policies; these may concern any regulations or situations for which the Research Center Teacher feels that an expression of student opinion provides the most constructive way to formulate workable policies. Obtaining student opinion may be done in any of several ways, depending in part on the philosophy and organization of the school. Student Research Center assistants should be given opportunity to express opinions about Research Center policy and procedures. A student Research Center committee forms an excellent aid for the Research Center and provides good social experiences for its members. In general, only matters of major concern involving students and the Research Center are handled by the student government.

The availability of Research Center space for display purposes should be made known to teachers, class advisers and officers of student groups. By means of these displays, the students become acquainted with the work, interests and activities of individual students in and out of school, or of class or club groups.

The Research Center should provide opportunities for at least one group project each year. These activities enable students to work together in a group, to make plans, and to carry a project to its successful completion.

Student assistants who are not paid should spend a major portion of their time on those activities that have some educational value. If no student assistants are paid, the policy should be followed to plan their program of Research Center activities so that all students have some opportunity to carry on some work that has educational value. The time of a student Research Center assistant should not be exploited to the extent that his work is concerned only with the repetition of simple mechanical tasks.

Rewards for student Research Center assistants should be consistent with that given for other school services performed by students. Students might receive recognition along with other school honors; activity points or school citizenship points might be awarded. If the school has a work program for young people, then Research Center assistants should be paid for such non-

Appendix: Criteria for Evaluation

educational aspects of the Research Center work as shelving. It is recommended that students do *not* receive a academic credit for working in the Research Center.

The School Research Center Teacher needs a knowledge of all phases of reading in order to participate effectively in the reading program of the school.

The Research Center has significant contributions to make to the school's program of social guidance and the school Research Center Teacher should be providing services.

While teachers and the Research Center Teacher both share in giving various kinds of library instruction, the school Research Center Teacher must assume the responsibility for the program as a whole.

An introductory orientation lesson (usually the equivalent of two class periods) should be given by the school Research Center Teacher to all new students; this should deal with the arrangement of the Research Center, Research Center rules and services, and a general introduction to the card catalog, the classification plan of the Research Center and the most basic reference books.

All instruction other than organization should be given by the teachers at the time it is needed in each of the various subject fields. The school Research Center Teacher and teachers should plan together to integrate such instruction. The instruction should be a continuous and systematic process from elementary school through college since proficiency cannot be fully developed in any one grade or level in any one subject.

By having a committee, systematic provision is made for the introduction of instruction on the use of the Research Center and its resources in the classes. The major task of this committee is to decide what types of knowledge and skills should be required of the students at each grade level, and to see that this instruction is provided. The school Research Center Teacher should serve as chairman of the committee. In schools where curriculum study or revision is taking place, the Research Center Teacher should indicate where instruction in the use of Research Center resources can be integrated in the various subject fields.

Results of Research Center instruction should be tested to measure the development of the students' ability to use books and

Research Centers so that further instruction may be provided on the basis of the needs of individual students. Many schools prefer to construct their own tests. Tests which are widely used can be obtained from the California Test Bureau, Los Angeles, and the Educational Publishers, Nashville, Tennessee.

Students should be familiar with these other Research Center resources. The school Research Center Teacher should assume the responsibility for making other Research Center services known to students.

A functional school Research Center program shows continuous service. While it is not possible to evaluate the Research Center's service in these areas on the basis of the numerical frequency with which they occur, a check made once a year gives the Research Center Teacher some indication of the general pattern of these services to students and the degree to which they are being provided satisfactorily.

Records of this type provide the school Research Center Teacher with useful evidence in selecting books and other materials for the Research Center, and in evaluating the adequacy of Research Center space and size of Research Center staff. It is frequently more illuminating to note what educational services the Research Center Teacher could not perform (through no fault of his own) than to detail what has been done.

Communication by the Research Center Teacher proves useful to teacher, students and Research Center Teacher. In schools where anecdotal records are kept, the Research Center Teacher participates in this activity along with other teachers in the school. In schools where students have scheduled Research Center periods, the Research Center Teacher makes a report (of the same general type used by subject teachers) for each student. In other situations, limitations of time will probably mean that the Research Center Teacher can report observations on students only in extreme cases (both negative and positive).

In order to provide satisfactory Research Center service for teachers and students, the Research Center Teacher needs to be informed reasonably far in advance about assignments to be made or units to be taught. In the case of new units, it is well for teachers and Research Center Teachers to discuss the accessibility

Appendix: Criteria for Evaluating 135

of Research Center resources while the unit is still in the planning stage. By this means, new materials may be purchased or secured in advance. Sometimes the unit may have to be modified in terms of lack of available materials or in terms of the reading levels of the students.

It is the responsibility of the administrator to encourage teachers to keep the Research Center Teacher informed about class assignments.

All faculty members have the responsibility and should have the opportunity for cooperating with the Research Center Teacher in the selection of books in their subject fields. The department heads, if there are such, assume major responsibility for the teachers in that department. The final responsibility for the selection of all materials for the Research Center rests with the Research Center Teacher in order to avoid unnecessary duplication and to maintain balance within the collection.

The school Research Center should be open a half-hour before school; it should be open during all periods of the school day, including the lunch hour, and open after school for at least the length of one period unless all students leave by bus.

The School Research Center Teacher should be familiar with the other Research Center facilities in the community which are available to young people during summer vacation. The Research Center Teacher should make these resources known to the students. School Research Centers should remain open during the summer in communities where other Research Center facilities are lacking or inadequate. *Sufficient clerical help and professional staff must be provided for this service.*

The school Research Center should follow a liberal policy of lending materials for use during vacation periods.

If less than 75 percent of all the students in the school are using the Research Center during a typical week, or if the median percentage of the seating capacity used in the Research Center each period is less than 75 percent, the Research Center Teacher will want to inquire into the conditions causing these situations. Inadequate facilities (particularly space) may be one answer, and this fact should be discussed with the principal. Such casual factors as textbook centered instruction, or overcrowded school conditions that necessitate running the school in two or more shifts, or an instructional program that eliminates free periods for students, may result in a lack of Research Center use that becomes an overall problem for the faculty as a whole to consider.

The faculty should decide, in terms of the objectives of the school, to what extent they want students to use materials other than textbooks. In some schools, this question has been considered significant enough so that a special study was made in which such evidence as the following was gathered for a period of one semester: the number of free periods that students had and the pattern of these periods (i.e., whether they all came on the same day, etc.), the classroom collections and the type of use made of them, and the number, type and source of materials used by students. On the basis of the evidence thus gathered, the faculty discussed whether the students were meeting acceptable standards and, if not, what the school might do.

Attendance statistics are important and necessary only when they can be used to measure and to interpret service or needs of the school Research Center. It is not desirable that records of this type be kept daily throughout the school year; periodic samplings at reliable times are sufficient. If these records are broken down by grade level of students, qualitative as well as quantitative interpretations are possible.

Circulation figures should not be overemphasized, and gains or losses in circulation do not constitute in themselves a reliable measure of the success or failure of a Research Center program. Circulation figures for one school in most cases cannot be compared validly with those of another school.

The main values to be derived from circulation statistics are those that come from the interpretation or analysis of the statistics. For example, low circulation figures in nonfiction areas may signify a mediocre or inadequate collection of books in the Research Center in these fields.

Circulation figures are most useful when they provide some insight into the extent and nature of the reading of students. In order to serve this purpose, circulation records have to be quite detailed, and this involves more work than the Research Center

Appendix: Criteria for Evaluating

ordinarily has time for; consequently, the Research Center Teacher will keep detailed circulation records only at intervals—perhaps once every five years.

Toward Better Service

Evaluating the Library/Media Program of the Fort Knox (Ky) Dependent Schools

Thelma J. Estes, Coordinator for Instructional Media
(reprinted with permission of the author)

In the development of programs for independent study and research, the school media center has the opportunity, as never before, to come to the front and to assume its rightful role as the heart of the school. Out of the frustration of rigid scheduling, uninspired story hours, and endless bookkeeping it is emerging into the light of a new day in learning—the consideration of the student who has finally achieved the right to learn as an individual and to pursue knowledge as wide and as deep as his interest and his ability leads him. We are fortunate to have the support and the opportunity to further develop a program in our schools which will afford unrestricted research opportunities for all the students.

When the flexible program was first adopted, there was hesitation on the part of some administrators and rightfully so; but we have been able to prove its merits and have had support from these same administrators in encouraging the classroom teacher to cooperate. Now we are ready to offer a better program for *all* grades. Let us drop the word "schedule" because it is no longer appropriate; as all times during the day will be free for all students. We are aware that it takes some time to accustom ourselves

Appendix: Toward Better Service

and our patrons to any changes, but we have passed the first hurdle of allowing a free flow of students through the media centers and should be able to add some finishing touches such as more individual instruction, a deeper involvement in curriculum planning and enrichment, better rapport with faculty and students, and a wider knowledge of reference work at all levels.

As it is with any change, there are weaknesses in the program that would be well to examine with suggestions for improvement. You have, no doubt, discovered many of these on your own and have probably devised methods to correct them. Your own creativity and initiative is the key to the success of the program as it has been in the past and will always continue to be. Perhaps these suggestions will be helpful to you.

In order for a library program to be an integral part of a total school program of independent study, there are essentials that must be recognized:

1. The media center must remain flexible both in time and service.

Much has been said concerning flexibility for all educational programs in recent years. It would be difficult to provide reasonable service and library materials for individual students if the library had to close its doors to all others while a class or story hour was in session. Some of us are finding difficulty in allowing a free flow of students through the media center while such activities are in progress. Most of the time the problem is with the attitude of the librarian rather than the discipline problems created by the students. We cannot ask the classroom teacher for released time for individual study and research if the student will be stopped at the door and returned to the classroom because another activity is in progress.

Arrangement of library furnishings and facilities might provide part of the solution to this problem. Shelving and furniture may be grouped in an informal manner to mark off a section for story hours, committee work or special subject areas. Some of the Parent Teacher organizations have provided carpeting for the story area. Carrels to be used by individuals may be placed in the vicinity where social studies and sciences are housed, leaving the remainder of the library for group activities. Carrels or tables for audio-visual equipment may also be placed in hallways if library quarters are cramped.

Early in the term students should be familiarized with library arrangement and should be taught to proceed on their own if the librarian is involved with some program that should not be interrupted. Courtesy and good citizenship need to be emphasized so that disturbances are kept at a minimum. Media centers already under a flexible program are finding discipline problems fewer than under the traditional program.

"I'm just not going to have kids running out of the library while I'm doing a story" was one comment made by a librarian last year. The number of students who had interest in a project killed by this attitude is unknown, but it is certain that it happened to some. While interest is high is the time to look for answers. This could be the only time during the day a particular student may be free to come to the library. By the next day, the project could be completely forgotten and a librarian has satisfied her own wishes at the expense of destroying a learning situation.

If you are finding it difficult to maintain flexibility, ask yourself these questions:

A. Am I finding it difficult because I really don't want to be bothered?
B. Is there a way in which I could arrange time to be tied up less? Perhaps Parent Teacher Association could provide some clerical help.
C. Is the furniture arranged to the best advantage?
D. Is there space in the hallway that could be used?
E. Have I taught library useage effectively?

Satisfactory answers to the questions could solve many problems.

2. The media center should be as attractive and inviting as the surroundings allow.

Housekeeping has been poor in some of the media centers in the past. How long have those books been piled on the top shelf? Wouldn't that picture look better hanging than propped against the wall? Are magazines arranged so that they do not droop over the sections? All of these are minor details but they contribute greatly to the general atmosphere of the room.

Appendix: Toward Better Service

Books *will* get out of order if they are being used. Shelving is one of the constant chores of the librarian. Students in the upper grades, 3-12, may be taught to do an efficient job of this or your PTA volunteer willingly assumes part of the task. It is no great cause for alarm if the book cart becomes loaded frequently, but shelving should be done as time allows and as orderly as possible so that students are able to locate materials needed without the constant assistance of the librarian. Books replaced helter skelter on the shelves discourage the researcher after he has looked in vain for the title the card catalog says should be here. Picture books may be shelved in a general alphabetical arrangement, but all others should be arranged in shelf list order.

Many items may be used to improve the appearance of the media center. Pictures suitable for the schools are always attractive. Wall space is at a premium in our centers, but some well chosen pictures add much to the general appearance. It is well to change them occasionally if possible, taking care to see that the proper proportion is maintained. Art reproductions mounted on an easel are attractive and arouse interest in the students. A different picture each month may be exhibited and serves as motivation in finding out answers to such questions as:

A. Who is the artist?
B. What is the country of origin?
C. What makes this particular picture interesting?
D. Is this work typical of other works by this same artist?

Artifacts may be used in the same way to make the room more attractive and to create interest in the students.

The bulletin board has many uses among which is a decorative device used to give a message. It may be economical to put up a backing at the beginning of the year that may be used all year but it is boring. Students soon recognize the fact that only the message has been changed and it does not get the attention it should. Bulletin boards should be changed at least once a month and may show new books and materials recently added; news concerning library activities; or seasonal observances. They should convey some message pertinent to the subject and should be fresh and interesting. Students enjoy helping with this work. Some who have little interest in other activities are especially talented as artists and are quite creative.

A reasonable amount of plant life is attractive. Avoid plants that hang over shelves and prevent students from reaching the books. Primary children will not move them aside to reach the books thus causing a whole section to go unused. Plants that go through a molting season and lose all their leaves are particularly unattractive. It is not a good idea to use the media center as a winter greenhouse for your plants you normally keep at home. Unless you plan to take care of them properly, it is best to omit them entirely.

Your work room is just that—a place to work. Avoid huge piles of mending or unfiled magazines. Clutter can be diverting to a good work situation.

3. The collection of a media center should contain a wide variety of media and materials for the user.

As each patron goes about choosing a subject of interest to him, the collection will need to be broadened to cover almost every item of interest in the experience of the modern user. It is particularly in this area that one must be aware of all phases of materials that might be used in the schools. We are no longer "keeper of books" but the modern media specialist is a dispenser of all types of learning devices. Rid yourself of the phobia that any type of material other than books and magazines will contaminate the premises. This may seem ridiculous at first glance but the reluctance to accept newer forms of media becoming so prevalent in education is resisted by some librarians to this extent. It is impossible to keep abreast of the latest developments through books alone. They simply are not published this rapidly. Each media center has access to the *Readers Guide to Periodical Literature*. Learn to use it; then teach it to the students. This means, also, that the periodicals must be kept and organized. Space prohibits an unlimited collection but selected titles should be kept for five years. Secondary schools would need those best for reference. A possible list might be:

Arts and Activities
Education Digest
Elementary English
Grade Teachers
Holiday
Junior Review
Living Wilderness
National Geographic
Newsweek
Plays

Appendix: Toward Better Service

> Horn Book
> Ideals
> Instructor
> Junior Historian
> School Arts
> Today's Health
> Viewpoint

Each media center should maintain and use a collection of audio-visual materials: filmstrips, records, tapes, transparencies, pictures, maps and globes. Encourage the students to search for information in this media as well. Learning areas especially emphasizing the use of this media can be very attractive and useful. Equipment has been provided for use by the individual student. No longer can we justify a great expenditure of funds for such materials and keep them untouched by the student. We are finding that students use greater care in the handling of audio-visual materials than many teachers. Instruction should be given in the use of such materials and repeated on an individual basis when necessary.

The media centers have been organized with a basic collection very similar in content. Subject areas should be examined to be sure a well balanced collection is being maintained. Note areas of weakness and let your orders reflect these needs. It will be necessary to keep up with changes in the curriculum in order to supply much needed material when the program starts. Curriculum bulletins are usually several months in preparation when a major revision is being planned. There is really no good reason that materials should not be available at the very beginning of a new program.

4. The librarian should be pleasant and receptive to patrons at all times.

When it all boils down to basic facts, it is the librarian who makes the program successful or is instrumental in allowing it to fall flat. What is the attitude you reflect to the student? Are you always willing to help a student who doesn't quite know what he wants? Are you understanding with the student who "forgets" exactly where the Readers Guide is immediately following an extensive lesson on this subject? It is doubtful if we would be regular users of a library, if the librarian behaved as some of us have in the past. Many children, and especially young people, are sensitive to ridicule; yet this has been used with our

own students. A short curt answer intimidates the timid child and he is reluctant to expose himself again to this form of behavior. The atmosphere of the library depends upon you, the librarian.
- A. Learn the names of as many of the students as you can as soon as you can. Few people like to remain anonymous or to have to respond to "you—you over there in the red dress."
- B. Be willing to go beyond the confines of your own media center to obtain information. You may feel the subject is really not worthy of research, but this decision is not yours to make. It may be the most important work to this individual that he has done to date. Depending upon your attitude, it could very well be the first or the last research this student will do.

    Keep a lookout for pertinent information at home as you read the daily paper or your own magazines and be ready to share it with your students. Make a file for research topics to refresh your memory. It boosts a child's ego to be greeted by a librarian who has "a little information I found for your research topic."
- C. Establish rapport with students so that the atmosphere of the media center will be welcoming for them. A smile, a cheery "Good Morning" can do much to start the day off right. Students are likely to respond in a similar manner; and it makes the media center a pleasant place to work.
- D. It is not always essential that every student have a research topic to keep him busy. Some of the most effective library usage I have noted has been students "browsing" through the shelves. Encourage more of this recreational type of use. It is good to have a browsing center where the student may be undisturbed if space and furniture arrangement allows it.
- E. Keep the media center open at all times during the school day. If your principal agrees, students might be allowed to come to the library if they arrive at school a little early, or to stop by the library on the way home in the afternoon. It will be necessary for you to be there at these times. Try

Appendix: Toward Better Service

to arrange your lunch period to keep the media center open while your most frequent users are able to come. This may necessitate your eating a little early, a little late, or having a tray brought to the library. At any rate, do not insist on these privileges from your principal and then lock your library to have breakfast in the lounge or to visit your friends while frustrated students line up at the door.

F. Establish rapport with the faculty so that they will come to you rather than your having to seek them out:
   (1) Be sure that something constructive comes from your conferences with them. These conferences should be on a regular basis agreeable to you and the teacher. If you are requested to supply materials for a course of study, give it the best you have. Do not file it back and forget about it.
   (2) Give prompt service to any request. Let the teacher know it has not been forgotten by notifying her when material has been located for a particular group or individual.
   (3) Keep the daily paper in the media center. This might be one instrument to bring the teacher to you. While she is there to read the paper would afford a good time to discuss library needs for her class.

The media center should be the center of all activities in the school. Our motto might be "Think Library." Try to develop such an atmosphere and an attitude that a teacher or student who needs that little something extra or the basis for a whole unit of study will naturally migrate to the media center where help will be available. Much of the complaint has been that it is hard to get the teacher involved. Try some of these methods:

A. Listen for problems the teacher might have and offer to help. There might be a student who is needing extra help or one who is progressing far beyond the rest of the class. Offer to give these students individual attention.
B. If you are not invited to join team teaching planning periods, request permission to attend.
C. If the teacher will not come to you for conferences, look her up and invite her in person.

D. Always try to have something constructive to offer in the way of curriculum enrichment, time saving, or independent activities.
E. Be receptive to any ideas or suggestions.
F. Maintain a friendly, helpful attitude in the media center. You will soon find teachers and students seeking you out.

This may seem to be an ambitious program, and it certainly may be for the librarian who would like to spend her days in the seclusion of her workroom, typing catalog cards or sitting at the circulation desk stamping books and cards. We need to realize this type of library service is already passe'. In order to exist in the modern educational scheme we will need to trade one set of time worn values for another more progressive and far reaching. We have the flexible program we have been striving for; now it is up to us to see that it gives the type of program to fill the needs of our total curriculum. Everyone will be told that this is the program and it will be implemented. Now is the time to make it work. Good luck!

Selected Bibliography

The School Administrator
Adams, Charles W. "The School Media Program: A Position Statement." *School Media Quarterly* Winter 1974
Case, Robert N. "Criteria of Excellence Checklist." *School Libraries* Spring 1969
Darling, Richard. "I.M.C.-Library Services." *The Instructor* November 1967
Gibbs, Wesley F. "The School Library . . . An Administrator Speaks." *School Activities and the Library*. American Library Association 1966
Henne, Frances. "School Libraries as Centers for Learning Experiences." *NEA Journal* March 1962
Whitenack, Carolyn. "Educational Trends and Media Programs in School Libraries" *American Library Association Bulletin* February 1969

Volunteers, Para-professional and Professional Staff
Gaver, Mary. "Crisis in School Library Manpower—Myth or Reality?" *School Activities and the Library*. ALA 1967
Gaver, Mary et. al. "Problems in School Library Supervision" *ALA Bulletin*. February 1968
Improvement of School Media Programs Committee. "Toward Greater Flexibility" ALA 1972

Polette, Nancy. *In: Service-School Library/Media Workshops and Conferences.* Scarecrow 1973.

Shelburn, Shirley. "Stop Grieving Quietly: A Proposal for Meeting Staff Needs" *School Libraries* May 1968.

Sullivan Peggy. Ed. "Staff Development." *School Media Quarterly* Spring 1973

Budgeting

Miller, Ellen. "Sensible Steps Toward Library Automation." *School Library Journal* February 1972

Weiss, Dudley A. "The Librarian and the Purchasing Agent—The Librarian vs the Purchasing Agent—Which Should it Be?" *The Library Binder* June 1970

"Do Federally Funded Programs Really Work?" *School Media Quarterly* Summer 1973

"The Development of a Planning Process for Media Programs." *School Media Quarterly* Summer 1973

Censorship in the Elementary School

Broderick, Dorothy. "Censorship Reevaluated." *School Library Journal.* November 1971

Boyer, Paul. *Purity in Print.* Scribners, 1968

Harvey, James A. "Acting for the Children?" *School Library Journal* February 1973

Levine, Alan. "Impressionable Minds. . . . Forbidden Subjects." *School Library Journal* February 1973

Banach, William. "Intellectual Freedom and the Community." *School Media Quarterly* Winter 1973

Krug, Judith. "Intellectual Freedom and the Rights of Children." *School Media Quarterly* Winter 1973

Jones, Harry and Lawson, Ray. "Intellectual Freedom and Materials Selection." *School Media Quarterly* Winter 1973

Harvey, James A. Ed. "Intellectual Freedom and School Libraries: and In-Depth Case Study." *School Media Quarterly* Winter 1973

Selected Bibliography

Evaluation
Darling, Richard L. "Accountability: Notes Toward a Definition." *School Library Journal* November 1971
Martin, Betty. *Suggestions for the Media Specialist and His Role in the Instructional Program and Promoting the Use of the School Library/Media Center.* ALA 1969
Noon, Elizabeth F. "Accountability and Media Centers." *School Libraries.* Fall 1971

Index

accessioning, 37
accountability, 116
administrator
  attitudes, 44-45
  chief, 15-17
  qualities, 10-12
  types, 10-12
American Library Association, 46
Armstrong, William, 101

Bang, Bang, You're Dead, 101
behavioral objectives, 116
Betsy's Little Star, 29
bids
  developing, 73-74
  items, 74-75
  preparation, 75-76
Big Wave, 29
Bizzell, John, 79
Buck, Pearl, 29
budgeting
  equipment, 84-85, 87
  materials, 85-87
  related to service, 81-83
  staff, 81-83
Butson, Reva, 131

Caddie Woodlawn, 112
Cat and Mrs. Cary, 29

censorship
  example, 97-103
  groups, 104-105
Charlie and the Chocolate Factory, 112
Community resources, 95-96
computers, 69-72
criteria for evaluation, 129-143

Dahl, Roald, 112
Director of Purchasing, 66
district
  administration, 15-18, 44-45
  organization, 9
  politics, 9-10

equipment selection, 84-85, 87-89
ESEA II, 89-93
Estes, Thelma, 138
evaluation
  criteria, 128-143
  staff, 55-56
  student, 122-125

facilities, 22-23, 85-89
Farley, Stella, 79
Federal Programs, 89-96
  Grants, 92-96
Ferguson-Florissant School Dis-

trict, 79
field trips, 95
Fitzhugh, Louise, 101
Fort Knox Dependent Schools, 138-146
furniture, 74-76
  specifications, 75-76

Gaver, Mary, 45
George, Jean, 102
goals
  media center, 19, 80-84
guidelines
  for volunteers, 38-39

handbook
  volunteer, 18, 35
Harriet the Spy, 101
Haywood, Carolyn, 29
Hemingway, Ernest, 113
hiring procedures, 49-51

In-Service Training, 36-38
Julie of the Wolves, 102
job description
  librarian, 51-52
  paraprofessional, 62-64
  supervisor, 27, 52

Klein, Norma, 102
Knapp School Libraries Project, 46

librarian
  evaluation, 53-54
  qualities, 51, 53-54
Library/Media Center
  goals, 17-20, 80-84
  program, 47-48, 93-96
Library Supervisor
  activities, 61-62
  and materials selection, 112-115
  and school administrator, 10-14, 43-45
  as a salesman, 20-21
  initial tasks, 17-19

qualities, 8
relation to professional staff, 55-58
tasks, 27

manual, volunteer, 18, 35
Martin, Betty, 93
materials center
  equipment, 84-87
  facilities, 85-89
  program, 47-48, 93-96
  resources, 85-87
  services, 93-96, 81-84
  staff, 55-58, 79-81
materials collection
  organization, 18
  processing, 29-30, 35-36
  selection, 18
  volunteer preparation, 29-30
memos, 22-26, 47-48
Merrill, Jean, 30
Missouri State Department of Education, 44
Mom, the Wolf Man, and Me, 102
multi-session training, 36

objectives, media center, 18-19, 79-85
organization
  school district, 9-10

paraprofessionals, 61-64
Pippi Longstocking, 43
politics
  school district, 9-10
principals
  types, 10-12
  attitudes, 15-17, 44-45
priority list, 74-76
private schools, 91-92
processing, 29-30, 35-36
professional staff, 55-58, 79-81
purchase orders, 66-67
purchasing
  agent, 66-67
  procedures, 66-69, 73-79

Index

re-evaluation, books, 111-112
reports, 58-59

salesmen, 72-73
School District of Greenville County, 93-96
school district politics, 9-10
School Libraries, 46
School Media Quarterly, 46
selection
  materials, 18
  problem areas, 103-111
Service Center
  activities, 59-60
  staff, 61-64
Sourland, 101
space requirements, 85-89
staff
  evaluation, 55-56
  hiring, 49-51
  media center, 55-58, 79-81
  meetings, 56-58
  need for, 23-24
  requirements, 23-26
  scheduling, 54-58
  service center, 61-64

statistics, 126
student
  activities, 93-95
  evaluation, 122-125
  involvement, 94-95
Sullivan, Peggy, 46
Sylvester and the Magic Pebble, 112

teacher attitudes, 14-15
technical processing, 29-30, 35-36

Utica Community Schools, 131-137

volunteers
  and library supervisor, 30-31
  guidelines, 39
  handbook, 18, 35
  obtaining, 31-32
  rewards, 39-42
  scheduling, 38-39
  training, 36-38
  types, 32-34
Voyages of Dr. Dolittle, 112